First World War
and Army of Occupation
War Diary
France, Belgium and Germany

2 DIVISION
5 Infantry Brigade
Royal Fusiliers (City of London Regiment)
17th Battalion
15 November 1915 - 31 January 1918

WO95/1350/2

The Naval & Military Press Ltd
www.nmarchive.com
Published in association with The National Archives

Published by

The Naval & Military Press Ltd

Unit 10 Ridgewood Industrial Park,

Uckfield, East Sussex,

TN22 5QE England

Tel: +44 (0) 1825 749494

www.naval-military-press.com

www.nmarchive.com

This diary has been reprinted in facsimile from the original. Any imperfections are inevitably reproduced and the quality may fall short of modern type and cartographic standards.

© **Crown Copyright**
Images reproduced by permission of The National Archives, London, England, 2015.

Contents

Document type	Place/Title	Date From	Date To
Heading	2nd Division 5th Infy Bde 17th Battalion Royal Fusiliers 1915 Nov-1916 Dec		
Heading	17th R. Fusiliers Vol I Nov 15		
War Diary	Tidworth Hants	15/11/1915	16/11/1915
War Diary	Boulonge	17/11/1915	18/11/1915
War Diary	Gd. Hasard	19/11/1915	22/11/1915
War Diary	Thiennes	23/11/1915	23/11/1915
War Diary	Busnes	24/11/1915	25/11/1915
War Diary	Annezin Nr. Bethune	26/11/1915	28/11/1915
War Diary	Le Preol	29/11/1915	30/11/1915
Heading	2nd Div. 5th Inf Bde. 17th Battn Royal Fusiliers January 1916		
War Diary	Norrent Fontes	01/01/1916	18/01/1916
War Diary	Hingette	19/01/1916	26/01/1916
War Diary	Essars	27/01/1916	28/01/1916
War Diary	Village Line	29/01/1916	30/01/1916
War Diary	C I Subsection Front Line	31/01/1916	31/01/1916
Heading	2nd Division 5th Inf Bde. 17th Battn Royal Fusiliers February 1916		
War Diary	Islands Festubert	01/02/1916	03/02/1916
War Diary	Village Line Festubert	04/02/1916	07/02/1916
War Diary	Islands	08/02/1916	11/02/1916
War Diary	Les Chocquaux	12/02/1916	17/02/1916
War Diary	Manqueville	18/02/1916	26/02/1916
War Diary	Fosse 10	27/02/1916	27/02/1916
War Diary	Etonnoir Sector	28/02/1916	29/02/1916
Heading	2nd Division 5th Inf Bde. 17th Battn Royal Fusiliers March 1916		
War Diary	Coron D'aix Fosse.10.	01/03/1916	02/03/1916
War Diary	Calonne Sector	03/03/1916	19/03/1916
War Diary	Fosse.10.	20/03/1916	20/03/1916
War Diary	Beugin	21/03/1916	28/03/1916
War Diary	Hersin	29/03/1916	31/03/1916
Heading	2nd Division 5th Inf Bde 17th Battn Royal Fusiliers April 1916		
War Diary	Hersin	01/04/1916	02/04/1916
War Diary	Calonne Ricouart	03/04/1916	05/04/1916
War Diary	Therouanne	06/04/1916	08/04/1916
War Diary	Calonne Ricouart	09/04/1916	12/04/1916
War Diary	Hersin	13/04/1916	16/04/1916
War Diary	Trenches	17/04/1916	20/04/1916
War Diary	Supports	21/04/1916	24/04/1916
War Diary	Trenches	25/04/1916	28/04/1916
War Diary	Fosse.10	29/04/1916	30/04/1916
Heading	2nd Division 5th Inf Bde 17th Battn Royal Fusiliers May 1916		
Miscellaneous	D.A.G. 3rd Echelon	03/06/1916	03/06/1916
War Diary	Fosse.10.	01/05/1916	02/05/1916
War Diary	Trenches	03/05/1916	06/05/1916
War Diary	Supports	06/05/1916	10/05/1916

War Diary	Trenches	11/05/1916	12/05/1916
War Diary	Fosse.10	13/05/1916	18/05/1916
War Diary	Bruay	19/05/1916	21/05/1916
War Diary	La Comte	22/05/1916	31/05/1916
Heading	2nd Division 5th Inf Bde 17th Battn Royal Fusiliers June 1916		
War Diary	Estree Gauchie	01/06/1916	03/06/1916
War Diary	Camblain L'Abbe	04/06/1916	06/06/1916
War Diary	Trenches Berthonval	07/06/1916	10/06/1916
War Diary	Support Line	11/06/1916	14/06/1916
War Diary	Trenches Berthonval	15/06/1916	18/06/1916
War Diary	Camblain L'Abbe	19/06/1916	27/06/1916
War Diary	Trenches Carency	28/06/1916	30/06/1916
Heading	War Diary 17th Battn The Royal Fusiliers July 1916		
War Diary	Trenches Carency II	01/07/1916	02/07/1916
War Diary	Villers Au Bois	03/07/1916	06/07/1916
War Diary	Trenches Carency II	07/07/1916	08/07/1916
War Diary	Trenches	09/07/1916	09/07/1916
War Diary	In Support	10/07/1916	13/07/1916
War Diary	Maisnil Bouche	14/07/1916	15/07/1916
War Diary	Marest	16/07/1916	20/07/1916
War Diary	Vaux Sur Somme	21/07/1916	23/07/1916
War Diary	Happy Valley	24/07/1916	26/07/1916
War Diary	Trenches	27/07/1916	31/07/1916
Heading	5th Brigade 2nd Division 17th Battalion Royal Fusiliers August 1916		
War Diary	Trenches Support	01/08/1916	02/08/1916
War Diary	Reserve	02/08/1916	03/08/1916
War Diary	Waterlot Fm.	03/08/1916	03/08/1916
War Diary	Front Line	04/08/1916	04/08/1916
War Diary	Waterlot Fm.	05/08/1916	06/08/1916
War Diary	Reserve	07/08/1916	09/08/1916
War Diary	Meaulte	10/08/1916	10/08/1916
War Diary	Ville Sur Ancre	11/08/1916	13/08/1916
War Diary	Picquigny	14/08/1916	16/08/1916
War Diary	Flesselles	17/08/1916	17/08/1916
War Diary	Bus	18/08/1916	19/08/1916
War Diary	Trenches	20/08/1916	22/08/1916
War Diary	Bus	23/08/1916	23/08/1916
War Diary	Coigneux	24/08/1916	29/08/1916
War Diary	Trenches	30/08/1916	31/08/1916
Heading	2nd Division 5th Inf Bde 17th Battn Royal Fusiliers September 1916		
War Diary	Trenches	01/09/1916	05/09/1916
War Diary	Reserve	06/09/1916	09/09/1916
War Diary	Trenches	10/09/1916	16/09/1916
War Diary	Coigneux	17/09/1916	19/09/1916
War Diary	Vauchelles	20/09/1916	30/09/1916
Heading	2nd Division 5th Inf Bde 17th Battn Royal Fusiliers October 1916		
War Diary	Vauchelle	01/10/1916	01/10/1916
War Diary	Bus	02/10/1916	02/10/1916
War Diary	Mailly Maillet	03/10/1916	06/10/1916
War Diary	Serre Section	07/10/1916	08/10/1916
War Diary	Leanvillers	09/10/1916	17/10/1916
War Diary	Mailly Maillet	18/10/1916	24/10/1916

War Diary	Mailly	24/10/1916	30/10/1916
Heading	2nd Division 5th Inf Bde 17th Battn Royal Fusiliers November 1916		
War Diary	Argueves	01/11/1916	30/11/1916
Heading	2nd Division 5th Inf Bde 17th Battn Royal Fusiliers December 1916		
War Diary	Maison Ponthieu	01/12/1916	31/12/1916
Heading	2nd Division 5th Infy Bde 17th Battalion Royal Fusiliers 1917 Jan-1918 Jan To 6 Bde-2 Div		
Miscellaneous	5th Brigade 2nd Division 17th Battalion Royal Fusiliers January 1917		
War Diary	Maison Ponthieu	01/01/1917	08/01/1917
War Diary	Gezaincourt	09/01/1917	10/01/1917
War Diary	Val De Maison	11/01/1917	11/01/1917
War Diary	Robempre	12/01/1917	12/01/1917
War Diary	O Villers	13/01/1917	16/01/1917
War Diary	Front Line	17/01/1917	20/01/1917
War Diary	Bouzincourt	21/01/1917	27/01/1917
War Diary	Bruce Huts	28/01/1917	31/01/1917
Heading	5th Brigade 2nd Division 17th Battalion Royal Fusiliers February 1917		
War Diary	Ovillers	01/02/1917	05/02/1917
War Diary	Front Line	06/02/1917	09/02/1917
War Diary	Wolfe Huts	10/02/1917	13/02/1917
War Diary	Front Line	14/02/1917	15/02/1917
War Diary	Bouzincourt	16/02/1917	16/02/1917
War Diary	Ovillers	17/02/1917	17/02/1917
War Diary	Bouzincourt	18/02/1917	18/02/1917
War Diary	Albert	19/02/1917	23/02/1917
War Diary	Front Line	24/02/1917	27/02/1917
War Diary	Support	28/02/1917	28/02/1917
Miscellaneous	Report On Raid On Enemy Trench At R.12.c.95.15 And Sap, By 17th Batt. Royal Fusiliers At 8.5 p.m. On 10th Feb 1917	11/02/1917	11/02/1917
Miscellaneous	Battalion Order No. 17/R/3	10/02/1917	10/02/1917
Miscellaneous	Code For 10.2.17		
Miscellaneous	Artillery Programme		
Miscellaneous	Formation For Advance		
Miscellaneous	Brief Summary of Information Regarding Raid	11/02/1917	11/02/1917
Miscellaneous	2nd Division	13/02/1917	13/02/1917
Miscellaneous	2nd Division	11/02/1917	11/02/1917
Miscellaneous	5th Bde	12/02/1917	12/02/1917
Heading	5th Brigade 2nd Division 17th Battalion Royal Fusiliers March 1917		
War Diary	Courcelette	01/03/1917	03/03/1917
War Diary	Albert	04/03/1917	10/03/1917
War Diary	Ovillers Huts	11/03/1917	15/03/1917
War Diary	Courcelette	15/03/1917	19/03/1917
War Diary	Ovillers Huts	20/03/1917	21/03/1917
War Diary	Hedauville	22/03/1917	24/03/1917
War Diary	Rubempre	25/03/1917	26/03/1917
War Diary	Gezaincourt	27/03/1917	27/03/1917
War Diary	Nuncq	28/03/1917	28/03/1917
War Diary	Croix	29/03/1917	30/03/1917
War Diary	Pernes	31/03/1917	31/03/1917

Heading	5th Brigade 2nd Division 17th Battalion Royal Fusiliers April 1917		
War Diary	Pernes	01/04/1917	08/04/1917
War Diary	Frevillers	09/04/1917	09/04/1917
War Diary	Maroeuil	10/04/1917	10/04/1917
War Diary	In The Line	11/04/1917	30/04/1917
Heading	5th Brigade 2nd Division 17th Battalion Royal Fusiliers May 1917		
War Diary	Kleeman Stellung Trench	01/05/1917	03/05/1917
War Diary	Ecoivres	03/05/1917	04/05/1917
War Diary	Cambligneul	04/05/1917	04/05/1917
War Diary	Dieval	05/05/1917	16/05/1917
War Diary	Ecoivres	17/05/1917	17/05/1917
War Diary	Hull Camp G 10 b	18/05/1917	18/05/1917
War Diary	Hull Camp	19/05/1917	23/05/1917
War Diary	In The Line	24/05/1917	27/05/1917
War Diary	In The Field	27/05/1917	31/05/1917
War Diary	In The Line	31/05/1917	31/05/1917
Heading	5th Brigade 2nd Division 17th Battalion Royal Fusiliers June 1917		
War Diary	Arleux en Gohelle	01/06/1917	01/06/1917
War Diary	Hull Camp	03/06/1917	03/06/1917
War Diary	Anzin St Aubin	04/06/1917	10/06/1917
War Diary	Railway Embankment Bailleul	11/06/1917	13/06/1917
War Diary	Budbrooke Camp	14/06/1917	17/06/1917
War Diary	Mont St Eloy	19/06/1917	19/06/1917
War Diary	Bethune	20/06/1917	20/06/1917
War Diary	Canal Left	21/06/1917	30/06/1917
Heading	5th Brigade 2nd Division 17th Battalion Royal Fusiliers July 1917		
War Diary	Canal Left (Pont Fixe)	01/07/1917	15/07/1917
War Diary	Le Preol	16/07/1917	21/07/1917
War Diary	Canal Left (Pont Fixe)	22/07/1917	31/07/1917
Heading	5th Brigade 2nd Division 17th Battalion Royal Fusiliers August 1917		
War Diary	Canal Section	02/08/1917	02/08/1917
War Diary	Le Preol	03/08/1917	08/08/1917
War Diary	Canal Section	08/08/1917	13/08/1917
War Diary	Le Preol	14/08/1917	20/08/1917
War Diary	Canal Section	20/08/1917	20/08/1917
War Diary	Kingsclere	26/08/1917	26/08/1917
War Diary	Canal Section	29/08/1917	29/08/1917
Heading	5th Brigade 2nd Division 17th Battalion Royal Fusiliers September 1917		
War Diary	Canal Left	01/09/1917	04/09/1917
War Diary	Le Preol	05/09/1917	08/09/1917
War Diary	Canal Left	09/09/1917	11/09/1917
War Diary	Bde Reserve	14/09/1917	19/09/1917
War Diary	Canal Left	22/09/1917	26/09/1917
War Diary	Beuvry	26/09/1917	28/09/1917
War Diary	Le Preol	29/09/1917	30/09/1917
Miscellaneous	5th Brigade 2nd Division 17th Battalion Royal Fusiliers October 1917		
War Diary	Le Preol	01/10/1917	04/10/1917
War Diary	Canal Left	04/10/1917	06/10/1917
War Diary	Bethune	07/10/1917	08/10/1917

War Diary	Lapugnoy	09/10/1917	31/10/1917
Heading	5th Brigade 2nd Division 17th Battalion Royal Fusiliers November 1917		
War Diary	Lapugnoy	01/11/1917	05/11/1917
War Diary	Thiennes	06/11/1917	06/11/1917
War Diary	St Sylvestre Cappel	07/11/1917	07/11/1917
War Diary	Zermezeele	08/11/1917	14/11/1917
War Diary	Winnezeele	15/11/1917	22/11/1917
War Diary	Night	22/11/1917	23/11/1917
War Diary	Beaulencourt	23/11/1917	23/11/1917
War Diary	La Bucquiere	25/11/1917	25/11/1917
War Diary	Hermies	26/11/1917	26/11/1917
War Diary	Burton Wood	27/11/1917	30/11/1917
War Diary	Front Line	30/11/1917	30/11/1917
Miscellaneous	P.A With War Of 17 R. Fusiliers Diary	01/12/1917	01/12/1917
Miscellaneous	17/Royal Fusiliers-Cambrai 1917		
Heading	5th Brigade 2nd Division 17th Battalion Royal Fusiliers December 1917		
War Diary	Old British Front Line	01/12/1917	02/12/1917
War Diary	Lock 6	03/12/1917	07/12/1917
War Diary	Front Line	07/12/1917	09/12/1917
War Diary	Labucquiere	10/12/1917	11/12/1917
War Diary	Hermies	14/12/1917	19/12/1917
War Diary	Front Line	20/12/1917	20/12/1917
War Diary	West Of Canal In Cambrai Sector	20/12/1917	21/12/1917
War Diary	Front Line	22/12/1917	26/12/1917
War Diary	Sanders Camp	27/12/1917	31/12/1917
Heading	5th Brigade 2nd Division 17th Battalion Royal Fusiliers January 1918		
War Diary	Sanders Camp	01/01/1918	03/01/1918
War Diary	Beaulencourt C Camp	04/01/1918	10/01/1918
War Diary	Jericho Camp	11/01/1918	12/01/1918
War Diary	Beaulincourt Jericho Camp	13/01/1918	22/01/1918
War Diary	Support Battn La Vacquerie Left	23/01/1918	25/01/1918
War Diary	Right Battn Left Brigade La Vacquerie	25/01/1918	28/01/1918
War Diary	Metz	29/01/1918	30/01/1918
War Diary	Divisional Reserve Metz	30/01/1918	31/01/1918

2ND DIVISION
5TH INFY BDE

17TH BATTALION
ROYAL FUSILIERS.
JAN — DEC 1916.
1915 Nov — 1916 DEC

Box 1350

2nd 33rd Hussain

Transferred to 2nd Dos Nov 25th with rest of 99th Regt.

121/7624

17th R. Fusiliers
Vol I

Nov. 15.

Army Form C. 2118.

WAR DIARY
or
INTELLIGENCE SUMMARY.
(Erase heading not required.)

Instructions regarding War Diaries and Intelligence Summaries are contained in F.S. Regs., Part II. and the Staff Manual respectively. Title pages will be prepared in manuscript.

Place	Date	Hour	Summary of Events and Information	Remarks and references to Appendices
	1915			
Tidworth HANTS.	15th/11	4.15 am	Advance party 4 officers 122 other ranks with all transport entrained for SOUTHAMPTON in order to proceed to HAVRE	Lin ex
Tidworth HANTS.	16/11	7.15 am	Right half Battalion entrained for FOLKESTONE — Left half battalion entrained at 7.20 am — Total battalion 27 officers 872 other ranks — Battalion complete less advance party — T.C.S.M. Murphy "D" Coy left behind ill in hospital — Arrived FOLKESTONE 12.30 — embarked leaving 12.30 pm arrived BOULOGNE about 3 pm — marched to OSTROHOVE rest camp - twent mile camp	Lin ex
BOULOGNE	17/11	—	At OSTROHOVE rest camp	Lin ex
ditto	18/11	12 night	Entrained at PONT des BRICQUES station — picking up transport at this point — arrived STEEN BECQUE station 4.30 pm — marched into billets at Gd. HASARD (MORBECQUE NORD) Strength 31 officers 994 other ranks; also 28 Divisional Band attached.	Lin ex
Gd. HASARD	19/11	—	In billets	Lin ex
ditto	20/11	—	In billets	Lin ex
ditto	21/11	—	In billets — Major Genl. GOUGH (G.O.C. 2nd Corps 1st Army) inspected battalion in billets.	Lin ex
ditto	22/11	9 am	Battalion marched to THIENNES arriving about 12 midday — went into billets	Lin ex
THIENNES	23/11	9 am	Marched to BUSNES arriving about 1.30 pm — went into billets	Lin ex
BUSNES	24/11	—	In billets at BUSNES	Lin ex

WAR DIARY
or
INTELLIGENCE SUMMARY.
(Erase heading not required.)

Army Form C. 2118.

Place	Date	Hour	Summary of Events and Information	Remarks and references to Appendices
BUSNES	1915 25/11	9 a.m.	Marched to ANNEZIN near BETHUNE arriving about 12.15 p.m. — The 99th Infantry Brigade were today transferred to 2nd Division from 33rd Division — Our Battalion 30 in all returned to 33rd Division (instruments returned to Battalion) — we sent into billets — Battalion strength 31 officers 990 other ranks — 4 men in hospital 100 Transport Line	
ANNEZIN Nr BETHUNE	26/11	—	In billets at ANNEZIN — Major General MURRAY. V.C. (G.O.C. 2nd Division) visited Officers in 42	
ditto	27/11	—	In billets at ANNEZIN	
ditto	28/11	6 a.m.	Battalion marched to LE PRÉOL and was attached to 5th Brigade for instruction in trench warfare etc. — 4 officers 96 N.C.O each from A & B Companies went for 24 hour tour of duty in trenches (attached 2nd H.L.I. & 1st Queens respectively) — 2nd Division bombardment ordered from 10 a.m. to 3.30 p.m. to the centre was by R.F.A. during night — Battalion in billets at LE PREOL under instruction future of Officers & NCOs detailed from 2nd H.L.I.	
LE PREOL	29/11		Battalion in billets — Parties from A & B reported back — no casualties — Smith parties from C & D Companies together with Lieut WOOTTON (Transport officer) half the machine gunners & half the signallers proceeded on return in the trenches — Bombardment ordered by 2nd Division from 10 a.m - 3.30 p.m	

2353 Wt. W2514/1454 700,000 5/15 D. D. & L. A.D.S.S./Forms/C.2118.

Army Form C. 2118.

WAR DIARY
or
INTELLIGENCE SUMMARY.
(Erase heading not required.)

Instructions regarding War Diaries and Intelligence Summaries are contained in F.S. Regs., Part II and the Staff Manual respectively. Title pages will be prepared in manuscript.

Place	Date	Hour	Summary of Events and Information	Remarks and references to Appendices
LE PRÉOL	1915 30/11		Signallers & machine gunners reported back – no casualties – A & B companies proceeded to the trenches for a 24 hour tour with the 2nd Oxford & Bucks. L.I. & the 10th H.L.I. respectively. C & D Company (Aberdeens) reported back – no casualties – a further section of machine gunners went into the trenches.	
	30-11-15		LE PREOL	

2nd Div.

5th Inf Bde.

17th BATTN ROYAL FUSILIERS

JANUARY 1916

Army Form C. 2118

WAR DIARY
or
INTELLIGENCE SUMMARY.

17th (Service) Bn Royal Fusiliers

(Erase heading not required.)

Instructions regarding War Diaries and Intelligence Summaries are contained in F. S. Regs., Part II. and the Staff Manual respectively. Title pages will be prepared in manuscript.

Place	Date	Hour	Summary of Events and Information	Remarks and references to Appendices
NORRENT FONTES	1916 Jan 1st		In billets - weather fine	
do	2nd		do	
do	3rd		do	
do	4th		do - Battalion inspected at work (by companies) by G.O.C. 2nd Brigade (Brig Gen WALKER V.C.)	
do	5th		do	
do	6th		do	
do	7th		do	
do	8th		do	
do	9th		do	
do	10th		do	
do	11th		do	
do	12th		do	
do	13th		do	
do	14th		do - Lieut Colonel C.G. HIGGINS awarded D.S.O.	
do	15th		do	
do	16th		do - weather wet	

2353 Wt. W2511/1454 700,000 5/15 D.D. & L. A.D.S.S./Forms/C. 2118.

Army Form C. 2118.

WAR DIARY
or
INTELLIGENCE SUMMARY. 17th (service) Battn Royal Fusiliers
(Erase heading not required.)

Place	Date	Hour	Summary of Events and Information	Remarks and references to Appendices
	1916			
NORRENT- FONTES	Jan 19	—	Battalion in billets – weather fine.	See etc
do	Jan 16th	—	Battalion in occupied billets (and of 9 divisional area) – and proceeded to LILLERS, where they entrained for BETHUNE – marched from BETHUNE to billets at HINGETTE – weather wet	See etc
HINGETTE	19th	—	5th Brigade in reserve – Battalion in Billets – weather fine.	See etc
do	20th		Battalion in billets – weather fine	See etc
do	21st		do	See etc
do	22nd		do – weather wet	See etc
do	23rd		do – do fair	See etc
do	24th		do – weather fine	See etc
do	25th		do	See etc
do	26th		Battalion evacuated billets and proceeded to billets at ESSARS – weather fine	See etc
ESSARS	27th		In billets – stand to arms 6.15 am – weather fine	See etc
do	28th		Battalion stood to arms 6.15 am. Battalion examined billets and paraded to march to the "VILLAGE LINE" – (i.e. FESTUBERT and L'EPINETTE – weather fine	See etc
VILLAGE LINE	29th		Battalion in billets – stood to arms 6.15 am – situation normal – battalion marched 3.30 pm to 5 pm – nothing further sent to front line – no casualties – weather fine	See etc

Army Form C. 2118.

WAR DIARY
or
INTELLIGENCE SUMMARY.
(Erase heading not required.)

17th (Service) Battalion Royal Fusiliers

Instructions regarding War Diaries and Intelligence Summaries are contained in F. S. Regs., Part II. and the Staff Manual respectively. Title pages will be prepared in manuscript.

Place	Date	Hour	Summary of Events and Information	Remarks and references to Appendices
VILLAGE LINE	30th		Battalion in billets - working parties all day in front line - Relieved 2nd OXFORD & BUCKS L.I. in front line C.I subsection at 7 pm - 17th MIDDLESEX REGT on right - and 2nd H.L.I. on left - no casualties - weather fine.	
C.I subsection front line	31st		Weather fine by day and night - slight shelling by enemy - machine guns and rifle fire (enemy) active - A & B Coys in front line C & D in support line - no casualties - weather fine.	

(Sgd) W.H. Cooke
Commanding 17th Royal Fusiliers

2nd Division
5th Inf Bde.

17th BATTN ROYAL FUSILIERS

FEBRUARY   1916

WAR DIARY or INTELLIGENCE SUMMARY

Army Form C. 2118.

page 1/ 1/5 (S) Battn Royal [?]

FEBRUARY '16

Place	Date	Hour	Summary of Events and Information	Remarks and references to Appendices
ISLANDS FESTUBERT	Feb 1st		Dispositions. 2 Coys in front line and 1 Coy in support. Enemy snipers fairly active. 2 men on No 3 ISLAND wounded by long range rifle fire. One of our Lewis Guns claims 3 to have hit a German who exposed himself to fire at our aeroplane. 2 patrols went out last night. Enemy heard hammering out trenches.	K
do	2nd		Enemy M.G.s fairly active during night. At 11/30 pm a few enemy trench field batteries ISLAND LINE and OLD BRITISH LINE. Patrols from right and Left Coys report enemy wire strong except opposite No 14 ISLAND. Noted pump full of mud	S.K.
do	3rd		Enemy Quiet except for occasional sniping. 1 Battalion was relieved by the 9th Oxford & Bucks L.I. as soon as it was dark, and proceeded to occupy the VILLAGE LINE. Westwards from Strongpoint Battalion battle H.Q. LE TOURET. Working party of 250 men supplied	S.K.
VILLAGE LINE FESTUBERT	4th		R.E.'s. "STAND TO" also takes place in VILLAGE LINE except in event of alarm	S.K.
do	5th		Working parties as before. Weather fine.	S.K.

WAR DIARY
or
INTELLIGENCE SUMMARY

Army Form C. 2118.

1/7 (S) Battalion Royal Scots (cont)

February (cont.)

Place	Date	Hour	Summary of Events and Information	Remarks and references to Appendices
	FEB			
VILLAGE LINE FESTUBERT	6th		Weather fine. Working parties as before.	
do.	7th		Battalion relieved the 9th and Black Watch after dark. Disposition as before.	
ISLANDS	8th		Our trench mortar battery fired a large number of bombs which the enemy replied with "whizzbangs". No casualties. Enemy active with rifle, minenos and trench mortars during the morning. Heavy shells heard bring down in vicinity of LE TOURET. Patrol went out at midnight and encountered enemy's working party 300 yards. Win found 5 houses strong and British bombs distinguished.	
do.	9th		Enemy sent up a number of green flares in early hours. Considerable activity on night. Support Coy. supplied wood (working party) to R.E. Weather fine.	
do.	10th		Enemy unusually quiet. Practically no firing or M.G. fire. Patrol failed to locate sufposed A mine was exploded in our right.	
do.	11th		Hostile working party fired on by Lewis gun at 3.30am.	

Army Form C. 2118.

WAR DIARY
or
INTELLIGENCE SUMMARY.

(Erase heading not required.)

Army Form C. 2118.

Page 3.

FEBRUARY (contd.) 17th (D) Battery R.F.A.

Place	Date	Hour	Summary of Events and Information	Remarks and references to Appendices
	FEB			
ISLANDS	11th (contd.)		Battalion was relieved by 17th MIDDLESEX after dark, and proceeded	
			to billets at LES CHOCQUAUX. Weather very cold.	
LES CHOCQUAUX	12th		In billets. Weather fine. Battalion inoculated.	
do	13th		do	
do	14th		do	
do	15th		do	
do	16th		do	
do	17th		Battalion received billets and proceeded to MANQUEVILLERS	
MANQUEVILLERS	18th		In billets	
do	19		do	
do	20		do	
do	21		do	
do	22		do	
do	23		do	
do	24		weather cold	
do	25		snow	

WAR DIARY
or
INTELLIGENCE SUMMARY.

(Erase heading not required.) FEBRUARY (cont.)

Army Form C. 2118

Place	Date	Hour	Summary of Events and Information	Remarks and references to Appendices
MARQUEUIL	26		Battalion executed billets and proceeded to FOSSE 10.	
FOSSE 10	27		Battalion moved up after dark and took over front line trenches 2½ coys	
			ETONNOIR SECTOR, 1½ coys in support. Weather	
			in front line, 1½ coys in support. Weather	
ETONNOIR SECTOR	28th		Front held about 500 yards. Enemy's distance	
			trench about 150 yards. Snowy front. Weather cold.	
do	29th		Snowy. Quiet. Weather cold.	

(signed) LtCol
Comdg 7th (Bn)

2nd Division

5th Inf Bde.

17th BATTN ROYAL FUSILIERS

M A R C H 1 9 1 6

WAR DIARY
or
INTELLIGENCE SUMMARY.

(Erase heading not required.)

Army Form C. 2118

Page I March 1915

Place	Date	Hour	Summary of Events and Information	Remarks and references to Appendices
CORONS DNYX @ POSS 2.10	MARCH 1st		9 little went on	
do	2nd		9 Wilts Battalion relieved 2nd Bn Bucks L.I. after dark in CALONNE RIGHT SECTOR. Dispositions 2 Coys and 1 Platoon in front line, 1 Coy and 3 Platoons in support.	S.A.
CALONNE SECTOR	3rd		Rifle grenades fell in + hit Reconnaissance made of German Ramparts rather weak and too close to parapet. Attempt made to push men nearer, but violent machine gun + rifle fire ensued. 2 N.C.O. and ... safe over + 1 Coy front from 1st N.T.R. moved night. Casualties 1 killed, 1 wounded.	S.R.
do	4-3		Left and Centre Companies relieved by 2nd N.B.F. Our Coy moved back at Caron's Farm Dispositions 2 Coys became platoons in Front line, 1 Coy and 1 Platoon in support, 1 Coy and 1 Coy in reserve. A few rifle grenades sent over our right. 1 wounded. Day very dull.	S.A.
do	5th			
do	6th		Rifle grenades fell on R front left. Attempt at bombing very feeble. Enemy rifle towards the day. Our Patrols sent out.	

WAR DIARY or INTELLIGENCE SUMMARY

Army Form C. 2118

17th (S) Battalion R.[?]

page II

MARCH

Place	Date	Hour	Summary of Events and Information	Remarks and references to Appendices
CALONNE SECTOR	6/3	6pm	Two enemy to sniper storm	S.R
do	7/3		Planes aft. private activity. No casualties	S.R
do	8/3		Patrol went through in 306 & A140 SOP, but returned without casualties and at 9pm. found patrol went out at 10.30pm. Owing to driving snow they could obtain no information. They were fired upon	
do	9/3		Enemy again threw out 6 grenades at SUPERINE SOP. Our own retal. party fired heavy trench mortar as they were seen damage to sap and trench A by actual hit to parapet. Patrol shrapnel or Lewis gun. An enemy. No damage to	S.R
do	10/3		A few battle grenades during the night. Our discov. a batt.[?] our own was not in hands. 2 patrols were out. Reply of enemy working on his trench.	
do	11/3			S.R
do	12/3		Enemy working party heard in SAP opposite JENNINGROD SOP. Our Lewis gun opened fire and fire would cease. 2 Patrols went out during the night. Evacuation of any enemy was not obtained.	

WAR DIARY
or
INTELLIGENCE SUMMARY

Army Form C. 2118

Page 5

1915 [?]

MARCH

Place	Date	Hour	Summary of Events and Information	Remarks and references to Appendices
DOUVE SECTOR	12th	(m.m.)	and Bregades so did th [?] 2 German exps picked up. A few hostile grenades. 1 man killed 1 wounded. Exploring an old communication trench occupied by [?] L/Cpl & capturing an old ammunition dump at 4th Sevens line. It involved a L/77 and a German sentry was killed at the [?] [?] [?] A German Volunteer was picked up showing the ayred [?] holding the line in future. IR Intermittent shelling day & night. A but qu[?]lam held SR	
	15th		Enemy shelled CORDON D'ARX Observat point. M. Bde M.G. Coy fired and [?] fire & [?] German trenches head at 3.50 am [?] [?] wounded S.R	
	16th		Enemy action with exception of sniping. Imm killed, 3 wounded. Enemy shells ROUSMARES. Deslapping of snow was probably only damage. Enemy aeroplane dropping [?] during day [?] on ROW23 [?] frequently shelled to harass SR [?] reinforcements.	
do	17th		General action with [?] [?] of [?] [?] and enemy trench mortar aid & Artillery [?] usual [?] [?] fire. SR	

WAR DIARY
INTELLIGENCE SUMMARY.

(Erase heading not required.)

Army Form C. 2118

Place	Date	Hour	Summary of Events and Information	Remarks and references to Appendices
CAGNIE SECTOR	17th (cont)		whole of range. 2 more bullets found in ground. Evidence of enemy snipers moving in advanced range of first portion of African patrol. Found it necessary to modify own snipers to be more recent with this from advance.	
do.	18th		Instituted shelling and cutting down places that advanced patrol was fired at. Keep own snipers established in advance.	
do.	19th		Bulls was claimed by 11th W. YORKSHIRE REGT and one by 2nd Bn. at FOSSE 10. Waiting for	
FOS.E.10	20th		Battalion ordered to billets at BEUVIN.	
BEUVIN	21st to 27th		Dr. HILLS. Wootton tunes.	
	28th		Battalion moved to HERSIN.	
HERSIN	29th 30th 31st		In Billets. Range overhead practice - each battn to have known Distance practice fire.	

2nd Division.

5th Inf Bde.

17th BATTN ROYAL FUSILIERS

APRIL 1916

Army Form C. 2118.

Sheet I 17th R. Fusiliers

WAR DIARY
or
INTELLIGENCE SUMMARY.
(Erase heading not required.)

APRIL.

Instructions regarding War Diaries and Intelligence Summaries are contained in F.S. Regs., Part II. and the Staff Manual respectively. Title pages will be prepared in manuscript.

Place	Date	Hour	Summary of Events and Information	Remarks and references to Appendices
	APRIL			
HERSIN	1st		In billets. Working parties furnished to R.E. & Weather fine. Enemy shelled the FOSSE and mine during midnight change.	S.O.
	2nd		Evacuated billets and proceeded to COLONNE RICOURT. Entrained at BRUAY, detrained at BRUAY, journey occupied 2 hours. Weather very warm.	S.O.
COLONNE RICOURT	3rd		In billets: weather fine.	S.R.
"	4th		In billets. Working parties provided for BOUVIGNY line. Weather fine.	S.R.
	5th		Evacuated billets and proceeded to THEROUANNE. Entrainment at COLONNE RICOURT.	
THEROUANNE	6th		RICOURT; detrainment at AIRE.	S.R.
	7th		In billets. Weather fine.	S.R.
"	8th		In billets. General Joffre went to manoeuvres. Weather fair.	S.R.
COLONNE RICOURT	9th 10th 11th		Evacuated billets and entrained to COLONNE RICOURT.	S.R. S.R. S.R.
	12th		In billets: weather fair. Batt: evacuated billets and moved to ST HERSIN. Entrainment BRUAY, detrainment HERSIN. Weather wet.	S.R. S.R.
HERSIN	13th 14th 15th		In billets. Weather wet & fair	S.R.

WAR DIARY or INTELLIGENCE SUMMARY

Army Form C. 2118.

Sheet 2.

17th R. Fusiliers

APRIL

Place	Date	Hour	Summary of Events and Information	Remarks and references to Appendices
	APRIL 16th		Proceeded to billets and relieved 11th WEST YORKSHIRES in ANGRES I. Intermix shelling by the enemy during the relief, two parties of 3 minutes each. One man wounded. General damage done to the trenches. A reconnaissance was made by our own and enemy parties in trying our work and now the parapet. Patrols report German working parts were M.G. fire was opened as our party came in.	S.R.
TRENCHES	17th		Work repairing parapets, laying track boards, building firesteps and revetments and clearing up support line. Enemy quiet.	S.R.
"	18th		Clearing up trenches. Enemy quiet except MG fire during the night. Made a few left bombs. Wiring party put up 69 coils.	S.R.
"	19th		Enemy quiet. Weather rainy & some mud. Wiring continued with 1 division and bad weather. We put up 100 up. Lunch 4-5 pm.	S.R.
"	20th		Battn. was relieved by 2nd Ox. & Bucks LT. 2 Companies moved billets in BOUY-GRENAY and two to MECHANICS E METROPOLITAN POSTS trenches. Weather fine.	S.R.

WAR DIARY or INTELLIGENCE SUMMARY

Army Form C. 2118.

Sheet 3

27th R. Irish?

Place	Date	Hour	Summary of Events and Information	Remarks and references to Appendices
	APRIL			
SUPPORTS	21st		Weather fine. Carrying parties &c.	S.R.
"	22nd		2 Coys in MECHANICS & METROPOLITANT relieved by 2 Coys from BUCKINGHAM.	S.R.
"	23rd		Weather fine. Carrying parties &c.	S.R.
"	24th		Relieved 2nd O. and Bucks L.I. in front line 9NGR3SI. 1 man wounded.	
			Sunny action with riffle grenades during relief. Patrols went out.	S.R.
TRENCHES	25th		Hostile riffle grenades during morning. To which STOKES gun retaliated.	
			Sunny whizzbangs on A Coy. 3 men wounded. Sunken	
			patrol bombed opposite R Coy. Our patrols sent out sounds of	
			shelling in Sunken Trenches. Wiring parties out all night.	S.R.
"	26th		Firing parties and boys exploded in TRENCHES and MOFTON [?]	
			Sunny very active with riffle grenades and whizzbangs, to which	
			we retaliated with riffle grenades and Trench mortars. 1 killed 2 wounded. S.A.	
"	27th		Enemy active with riffle grenades and Trench mortars. 1 wounded.	
			Test fire allowed 7 P.M. Enemy very quiet during night. Strong	
			wiring parties out all night.	S.R.
"	28th		Were relieved by 2 & 10x Bucks L.I. & not artillery activity or nm	

WAR DIARY
or
INTELLIGENCE SUMMARY.

Army Form C. 2118.

Sheet 4.

17th R. [Fusiliers]

APRIL

Place	Date	Hour	Summary of Events and Information	Remarks and references to Appendices
TRENCHES	April 28		night and left batteries 8 and 9 p.m. 6 red rockets were sent up opposite our left Coy at 8.30 p.m. and 2 green rockets 7.40 p.m. Enemy reported to be testing direction of wind. 8.30 p.m. by many another rockets. 1 killed, 4 wounded	C.R.
FOSSE 10.	29		In billets. Carrying parties etc. Weather fine	E.R.
	30		do. do.	E.R.

C.J. Hoppin Lt. Col.
Comdg. 17th R. Fusiliers

2nd Division.

5th Inf Bde

17th BATTN ROYAL FUSILIERS

MAY 1916

SECRET   17th Royal Fusiliers
3/6/16

D.A.G.
3rd Echelon

Herewith War Diary
for May 1916.

C R Kippins
Cmdg 17th R. Fus   Lt Col

Army Form C. 2118.

WAR DIARY
or
INTELLIGENCE SUMMARY.
(Erase heading not required.)

17th (S) Batt. R. Fusiliers

MAY

Places	Date	Hour	Summary of Events and Information	Remarks and references to Appendices
FOSSE.10.	MAY 1st		In billets. Weather fine.	S.R.
"	2nd		Left FOSSE 10 for trenches, ANGRES.	S.R.
TRENCHES.	3rd		Relieved 2nd O.R. and Bucks Bn. Lt. Inf. After heavy rifle grenades during the morning to which we retaliated. 29 rifle & rifle grenade trench gun fire in. Several working party. 2 patrols sent out during night. Enemy had anything.	10 O.R. wounded 1 O.R. 2 O.R. wounded S.R.
"	4th		Enemy trenches looked over by hours and trench mortar. German out run a number of rifle grenades and trench mortar 1 O.R. killed and 5 O.R. wounded.	1 Lt Bower Killed S.R.
"	5th		A quiet day. Enemy continue a few rifle grenades & what we have informaly. A patrol went out before dawn and lay up about between the lines. They did not see or hear anything. Made	1 C.
"	6th		A quiet day. Battalion moved back into support. 2 Coys in BULLY GRENAY and 2 in support trenches. 1- 2 O.R. wounded 143 work	S.R.
SUPPORTS.	7th 8th 9th 10th		of men put out in 4 days. In support. 100 men per day trained for work in the trenches. Relieved the 52nd L.I. in the line. Enemy shelled Guy-out Tr. in the afternoon	S.R. S.R. S.R.

WAR DIARY
or
INTELLIGENCE SUMMARY

Army Form C. 2118

Sheet II

1/7 2/8 Batt R.F.

Place	Date	Hour	Summary of Events and Information	Remarks and references to Appendices
	MAY			
TRENCHES	11th		Enemy whizbanged T front L/pr a few minutes in the morning	
			No rifle grenade activity. S.R.	
"	12th		Battn moved to billets at FOSSE.10 S.R.	
FOSSE.10	13th to 18th		In billets FOSSE.10. 250 men daily details for working parties.	
			Weather fine. S.R.	
	19th		Left FOSSE.10 and proceeded to BRUAY. E.R.	
BRUAY	19th		In billets. 350 men in working parties E.R.	
	20th		In billets. E.R.	
	21st		Left BRUAY for LA COMTE. E.R.	
LA COMTE	22nd 23rd		In billets LA COMTE. 3 men wounded in working party in 22 H.S.A	
	24th		Battn ready to move at 1 hrs notice owing to Sudden attack	
			on VIMY RIDGE. E.R.	
	25th		Battn left La Comte for ESTREE CAUCHY. E.R.	
	26th		In billets ESTREE CAUCHY. E.R.	
	31st		Weather was fine throughout. All moves done by road. E.R.	

[Signature] Lt Col
Comdg 1/7th R. Fus

2nd Division.

5th Inf Bde

17th Battn   ROYAL FUSILIERS

J U N E   1 9 1 6

Army Form C. 211

17th (S) Battalion
Royal Fusiliers

WAR DIARY
or
INTELLIGENCE SUMMARY

(Erase heading not required.)

Sheet 1.

JUNE

Place	Date	Hour	Summary of Events and Information	Remarks and references to Appendices
ESTREE GAUC HIE	June 1st		In billets. Weather fine. S.R.	
	2nd 3rd 4th 5th		Bns marched to CAMBLAIN L'ABBE. Took over billets from 23rd Royal Fusiliers S.R.	
CAMBLAIN L'ABBE			In billets. S.R.	
	6th		Relieved 2/2 Ox and Bucks L.I. in BERTHONVAL SECTOR. One A mining. 3 Coys in front line. 1 Coy in support.	
			Weather fine. Bombing quiet. S.R.	
TRENCHES BERTHONVAL	7th		Sunny & quiet. Large working parties were sent for front line during the night. They were at	2/Lt Jumsdale 1 O.R. wounded 1 O.R. killed
			work as men also had two days w'ing parties at. S.R.	
	8th		Sunny & quiet. A few shells fell in the ZOUAVE VALLEY. Some wiring working parties were	2 O.R. wounded
			again during the night. S.R.	
	9th		Situation quiet. Nothing working parties as per usual. S.R.	
	10th		Sunny and fine. From noon in the afternoon and dropped about 15 shells in ZOUAVE VALLEY	2 O.R. killed
			about 4 p.m. Bn was relieved by 4th Ox Bucks L.I. + moved into support at CABARET ROUGE S.R.	2/Lt Rumsden + 2 O.R. wounded
SUPPORT LINE	11th 12th 13th 14th		1 Coy at BRIDGE LINE. 1 Coy at GRENADIER TRENCH. 2 Coys + Batt HQ at CABARET ROUGE S.R.	
			In support. Harassing trenches. S.R.	
	14th		Batt relieved 2/Ox + Bucks in BERTHONVAL SECTOR. Enemy very quiet. Bn opened fire	
			with out on right front and fire on German working parties etc. S.R.	

Army Form C. 2118.

WAR DIARY
or
INTELLIGENCE SUMMARY.

(Erase heading not required.) VUDE.

Sht. 2.

17/3/Batt.
Royal Lancashire

Place	Date	Hour	Summary of Events and Information	Remarks and references to Appendices
TRENCHES BEATHONVAL	15.9		Enemy quiet. Slight enemy parties noticed by snipers. SL	
"	16.9		Situation quiet. Weather fine. SL	
"	17.9		Enemy dropped a considerable number of medium shells in and about DOUVE valley	SL around 9.0.
"			Between 1.30am & 2pm. Wiring parties much hampered by snipers 4L.	2 O.R. "
"	18.9		Some shelling by the enemy during the morning. Were relieved by 2nd S. Staffords in	1 O.R. wounded
			Regt. and Battn. moved to CAMBLAIN L'ABBE. Weather fine. SL	
CAMBLAIN L'ABBÉ	19.9 & 27.9		On Whit (date). Weather fine. Large working parties every other night. SL	
	27.9		Relieves 1st M.R. Rs in CARENCY SECTOR.	
			(2) Situation: 3 coys. front line & one in support	
			Weather wet. Enemy quiet. A gas attack appeared to be in progress on our left	
			from about 11.30 pm onwards, accompanied by great artillery activity. SL	
TRENCHES CARENCY	2.8.9		The RED Llama mine LIVEN BROADSTONE AND MILDREN CRATERS at 11.30 pm	L.T. SOMERSET
			L.T. SOMERSET commanding covering party of trenches were occupied was SL, and	2 O.R. killed
			13 others casualties were suffered during 20 minutes of severe bombardment by	13 wd
			the rest was successfully consolidated SL.	
	29.9		Enemy quiet. Weather fine. SL	
	30.9		Some artillery activity. Weather much warmer. SL	

5th Inf.Bde.
2nd Div.

WAR DIARY

17th BATTN. THE ROYAL FUSILIERS.

J U L Y

1 9 1 6

WAR DIARY

Army Form C. 2118

INTELLIGENCE SUMMARY.
(Erase heading not required.)

17th Royal Fusiliers

Vol I Sheet I JULY

Place	Date	Hour	Summary of Events and Information	Remarks and references to Appendices
TRENCHES CARENCY B	JULY 1st	12 noon	20 to 30 large MINNIES fell near support line of centre Coy. Howitzer battery retaliated. At night 6th R.B. (on our right) made a raid on hostile trenches. Our wire heavily shelled for 45 minutes 12.45am to 1.30am. No casualties. Weather fine	S.R.
"	2nd		In the morning some 20 to 30 MINNIES fell S of HOLLOWAY. Retaliated by Field Batteries. On right Coy front heavy snipers hit corner-post. Bells which S? Coy & Oxf Bucks & 5th Ox & Bucks twisted S. VILLERS-AU-BOIS. Weather fine. Cas. Nil. S.M.	
"	3rd		In little battle with TMs. S.R.	
VILLERS AU BOIS	4th & 5th		do. Weather fine. Raiding party rehearsed operation. Rev HOPKINS C.F.	
"	6th		Left VILLERS for the line (CARENCY II). Q.ms during night. S.R.	
TRENCHES CARENCY G	7th		On T.M. action in enclosure to support line for raid. Enemy retaliated & damaged HOLLOWAY & SUPPORT LINE. S.R.	
"	8th		At 1.5am a party of 70 men under command of Capt STEWART, Lt POLLOCK and Lt WOOTTON attempted a raid on hostile trenches opposite CENTRE PICQUET, KEEP Cox. A few men succeeded in entering the enemy trenches. P½ WHITE MAIN entered. Machine gun but was hit on the way back & he & some of his men left. STEWART reached German trench but was severely wounded. He was brought	

WAR DIARY or INTELLIGENCE SUMMARY

Army Form C. 2118

Sheet II

1/8 Royal Fusiliers (?)

Month: July

Place	Date	Hour	Summary of Events and Information	Remarks and references to Appendices
	8th cont.d		in by Cpl BOEHR who was awarded D.C.M. Capt STEWART and Lt WOOTTON (wounded) MILITARY CROSS. Lt WOOTTON was also wounded (shell). L/Corpl W. BACON missing. T.O.R. missing and 13 wounded. Other decorations awarded were Pte WHITE D.C.M. Pte WILTSHIRE, TRIMBEY and SHORCOCK MILITARY MEDAL. Lt ROPER MILITARY CROSS.	S.R.
TRENCHES	9th	8.30pm	Germans exploded a mine between PIOTOTH and BROADBRIDGE CRATERS. We consolidated new lip. Sept/Hastings with Pte CROWDER and WAGSTAFFE drove back 7 Germans who was [trying] round the left flank with bombs. The engt. awarded D.C.M. & 2 Ptes MILITARY MEDALS. Capt HYLE and Lt MEWITT wounded and 5 O.R. killed and 8 O.R. wounded. 2/Lt PECHELL was also wounded while on wiring in the early hours of the morning. Battalion was relieved by 2nd Bn. Bucks Lt. and moved into supports. Disposition: 1 Coy CRECY, 1 Coy CORONET ROUGE, 1 Coy in support, Rifle Brigade Bellis + 1 Coy in support Left Bellis. Batt. HQ in 2.30 pm at LEX Buttrin Pace S.R.	
IN SUPPORT	10th		In support. 1 O.R. wounded 1 O.R. killed	S.R.
	11th		In support. Weather fine	S.R.
	12th		"	S.R.
	13th		Left trenches for MAISNIL BOUCHE L.R.	

WAR DIARY or INTELLIGENCE SUMMARY

Army Form C. 2118

Sheet III

17th Royal Fusiliers

Month: July

Place	Date	Hour	Summary of Events and Information	Remarks and references to Appendices
MAISNIL BOUCHE	14th 15th 15th		In billets. Weather fair. ER	
MAREST	16th	6.19am	Left MAISNIL BOUCHE and marched to MAREST, about 13 miles. Weather fine. ER In billets. ER	
	20.2		Paraded 5.45 and marched to PERNES STN. Entrained there for SAULEUX. Arrival Saleux after 5 hours journey at 6.30 pm. Marched off again at 9.45 pm and arrived VAUX SUR SOMME 5.30 am. 15 mile march. ER	
VAUX SUR SOMME	21st 22nd 23rd		In billets. ER Marched from VAUX to HAPPY VALLEY, BRAY. Battn in bivouac. ER	
HAPPY VALLEY	24th		In bivouac. ER	
	25th		Left HAPPY VALLEY for the line (supports). Dispositions 1 Coy TROVES WOOD, 3 Coys LONGUEVAL ALLEY. Battn HQ in LONGUEVAL ALLEY. Germans bombarded men with "tear shell" and HE during relief. LT RICHMOND gassed. ER	
	26th	2.15am	Heavy bombing and rifle fire in DELVILLE WOOD for 15 minutes. Battn stood to. LONGUEVAL ALLEY shelled all day with shrapnel & HE. Casualties 3 OR killed, 12 OR wounded. Burning	
		10pm	commenced bombardment of BERNAFAY WOOD and gas shells at 10 pm. The continued all night with great intensity and without a break. 1 OR gassed. 4 patrols gave out at 4.13.3.0 Dart on our right. ER	

Instructions regarding War Diaries and Intelligence Summaries are contained in F.S. Regs., Part II. and the Staff Manual respectively. Title pages will be prepared in manuscript.

WAR DIARY or INTELLIGENCE SUMMARY.

(Erase heading not required.)

Army Form C. 2118.

Place	Date	Hour	Summary of Events and Information	Remarks and references to Appendices
TRENCHES	27th	7.40 a.m.	Attack on DELVILLE WOOD by 99th I. Bde. LONGUEVAL ALLEY heavily shelled. All communication with the wood broken.	
		11 a.m.	Arrival of runner from 2nd R. Inniskillings who stated that I. enemy was getting round their right flank. He brought a message to 22nd R. Fusiliers to come up on their right from N.E.	
		2 p.m.	A and B Coys moved up to DELVILLE WOOD by Capt. I.H. Bt.	
		2.15 p.m.	17th MIDDLESEX passed Batln. H.Q. on their way to DELVILLE WOOD followed by 2nd R. STAFFS. and 2 Coys 22nd Royal Fusiliers carrying S.A.A. and tools.	
		2.45 p.m.	24th R.F. advanced and up 100 lines deep. Shelling of LONGUEVAL ALLEY continued all day. Casualties Lt ROBINSON wounded, Capt RANSON's wounded. Capt KNOCKER R. 2/Lt PENNER killed. Lt ROSSITER killed. O.R. 16 killed. 90 wounded 7 missing. 2nd R.	
	28th		Tried to find front line. Battn H.Q. moved C N of BERNAFAY WOOD! B, C & D Coys reported in trenches W.N.E. edge of BERNAFAY WOOD. 2/Lt ... wounded lead to BRESLAU TRENCH the wood was shelled intermittently all day. Casualties	
			10 killed 13 wounded D. & I. missing. EC	
			2 + B Coys left DELVILLE WOOD at 6 a.m. 3rd R.	2nd Lt. RITCHIE/SOTTON 2 off killed
	29th		9 took over from 24th R. Fusiliers LONGUEVAL ALLEY. Bombardment commenced before dawn 6 wounded	2nd Lt. LE LIEVRE wounded

2353 Wt. W2544/1454 700,000 5/15 D.D.&L. A.D.S.S./Forms/C. 2118.

Army Form C. 2118

WAR DIARY
or
INTELLIGENCE SUMMARY.
(Erase heading not required.)

Sheet V

17th Royal ?

Place	Date	Hour	Summary of Events and Information	Remarks and references to Appendices
	30th	4.45 a.m.	Attack on GUILLEMONT and Trench E. of WATERLOT FARM. "C" Coy in position N end of LONGUEVAL with orders to move into ANGLE TRENCH when it was vacated by 24th R. Fus. immediately party this front, did not move out at all and Coy was under shell fire for 3 hours. The whole of the NORTHERN PART of LONGUEVAL was shelled all day. 2 known Coy in TRONES WOOD. Casualties. Lt UNDERWOOD killed. 2/Lt DAVIDSON and 2/Lt STABLES struck (Lt latter light) 3 O.R. killed, 42 OR wounded, Q.S. S.K. 3 known wounded & 2 known miss Coy 3rd Battalion.	
	31st		Somewhat less shelling than usual. We relieved Coy pt S.Z. = W S. poured on: (WATERLOT FARM) 3 O.R. killed. 1 S OR wounded. 12.	

C. Wyatt Lt Col
comdg 17th R. Fusiliers

5th Brigade.
2nd Division.

17th BATTALION

ROYAL FUSILIERS

AUGUST 1916.

WAR DIARY
or
INTELLIGENCE SUMMARY.
(Erase heading not required.)

Army Form C. 2118.

Sheet 1 Vol 10
AUGUST 1916   17th R Fusiliers

Instructions regarding War Diaries and Intelligence Summaries are contained in F. S. Regs., Part II. and the Staff Manual respectively. Title pages will be prepared in manuscript.

Place	Date	Hour	Summary of Events and Information	Remarks and references to Appendices
TRENCHES SUPPORT	Aug 1st		Battalion in support at LONGUEVAL ALLEY and 1 Coy in front line at INVERNESS COPSE, 1 Coy at TROVES WOOD. Battalion was relieved during the night and moved into camp between MONTAUBAN and CARNOY. A much needed day. Casualties 10. O.R. wounded.	
" RESERVE	2nd		Area was heavily shelled between 7am & 8am by medium field guns. Battn lost 1 at 8.20pm in front of B.H.Q. 1 O.R. wounded. Slept in huts.	
"	3rd		Up in own lines. Heavy hate. Battalion had carried 2 to food & water. On guns in front line. Battalion marched up and took over the front line at WATERLOT FARM at 4 AM. The Casualty rate during move 9.10 pm and 7pm. very slight commenced at 10 pm and lasted without cessation till dawn. Casualties 4 O.R. killed 9 O.R. wounded.	
" WATERLOT FM FRONT LINE	4th		Enemy shelled the area of the farm intermittently. Our guns keeping up fairly short normal quite close to our trenches. Area of TROVES WOOD was heavily shelled till midnight. A Night Trench dug along the supply running from S.E. Corner of DELVILLE WOOD on front 577AE.17.8.7 F.2.d.	

WAR DIARY
or
INTELLIGENCE SUMMARY.

(Erase heading not required.)

Army Form C. 2118.

Instructions regarding War Diaries and Intelligence Summaries are contained in F.S. Regs., Part II. and the Staff Manual respectively. Title pages will be prepared in manuscript.

Place	Date	Hour	Summary of Events and Information	Remarks and references to Appendices
PLATEAU PM.	5th		front running in east wall of the farm firing into trench 200 yards. got the man. The trench was occupied by 1 Coy before dawn, and they held it during the following day. Casualties 4 killed, 11 wounded. E.R.	
	6th		Enemy rather quiet. Casualties 1 killed & wounded. S.R.	
			Snipers were apparently operating in the new trench during the morning. Battalion was relieved by the 13th Essex Regt. No casualties except 2 wounded round 3 p.m.	
RESERVE.	7th		In reserve between MONTAUBAN and CARNOY. 2 Coys. advised up to German MONTAUBAN. village & keep. Casualties NIL.	
	8th		Battalion was under orders to move to the SANDPIT area MEAULTE. Orders cancelled at 6 p.m. and relay moved for Battalion to march to move up to the line the following day. Cas NIL. E.R.	
	9th	9 a.m.	nomic. E.R.	
MEAULTE	10th		The Battalion moved to the SANDPIT area MEAULTE. E.R.	
VILLE-SUR-ANCRE	11th		Battalion marched to VILLE SUR ANCRE (Brigade march) E.R.	
"	12th		In talk. Weather fine. E.R.	
	13th		Batt left VILLE and entrained at MERICOURT GARE for JASEUX. 3½ hours in train?	

Army Form C. 2118

Sheet III

17th R. Fusiliers

WAR DIARY
or
INTELLIGENCE SUMMARY.
(Erase heading not required.)

ACCCSR

Instructions regarding War Diaries and Intelligence
Summaries are contained in F. S. Regs., Part II.
and the Staff Manual respectively. Title pages
will be prepared in manuscript.

Place	Date	Hour	Summary of Events and Information	Remarks and references to Appendices
	13th	Cont	On arrival at SCEUX Battalion entrained and marched to PICQUIGNY 16 miles. ER	
PICQUIGNY	14th		In billets ER	
	15th		" ER	
	16th		Battalion marched to FLESSELLES ER.	
FLESSELLES	17th		Battalion marched to HENVILLERS [struck out] ER.	
BUS	18th		Battalion marched to BUS-LES-ARTOIS ER.	
"	19th		Battalion took over the front line from 1st Batt WELSH GUARDS near LA SIGNY FARM.	
PREVETES	20th		Sunny spirit. Disposition 2 Coys in front line + 2 Coys in support. Only small portion of 1st front line occupied; mainly held by combat posts and Lewis guns at heads of communication trenches. On our right flank where French relieved from aug. 10 in part of S.II 22 + 13th line no certain line known trenches were from 100 to 600 yards ER. Inspection arranged of front with view to put line 1 Coy to support. Battalion up to 5 to 200 line to trenches. Slight shelling flat's trench mortars in our left during the evening + intermittently — wiring parts out all night. 1 O.R. wounded	
	21st			

2353 Wt.W2544/7454 700,000 5/15 D.D.&L.   A.D.S.S./Forms/C. 2118.

Army Form C. 2118

WAR DIARY
or
INTELLIGENCE SUMMARY.
(Erase heading not required.)

17th R. Fusiliers

AUGUST

Place	Date	Hour	Summary of Events and Information	Remarks and references to Appendices
FRENCHES	22.8		Battalion HQ shelled intermittently. Enemy minnenwerfers & MGs active in neighbourhood from 9-9.30pm and 2pm to 10-10.30pm. Trenches considerably damaged. Our Arty retaliated rapidly. Shortly after 10.30pm a batch of bodies estimated strength 6 to 12 men entered our Rd front line post No SLABONY 19 and worked towards the town. Our post (Thos.) Shewe sharply challenged and came upon the hun firing bombs & the patrol made off. The Lewis gunner situated to cover this post Pte Maa.of them caused to freeze. Cpl. LOR Rideod 1st MARTIN also Lt CORWIN wounded. 3 O.R. wounded. SR. SQ.	
BUS	23rd		Batt[alio]n was relieved and returned to BUS. SQ	
COIGNEUX	24.8		Batt[alio]n marched to Coigneux. In billets.	
	25th		9½ hrs. Clout 350 Officers and men supplied nightly to carry up gas cylinders and explosives in the trenches at HEBUTERNE. Weather unsettled. SR.	
	26.8		"	
	27th		" 1 OR Killed, 3 OR wounded by a shell	
	28th		General when returning from carrying party. SR	

Army Form C. 2118.

WAR DIARY
or
INTELLIGENCE SUMMARY.
(Erase heading not required.)

Sheet V

17th R Fusiliers

AUGUST

Instructions regarding War Diaries and Intelligence Summaries are contained in F.S. Regs., Part II. and the Staff Manual respectively. Title pages will be prepared in manuscript.

Place	Date	Hour	Summary of Events and Information	Remarks and references to Appendices
COIGNEUX	29th		Battalion relieves 2nd Ox & Bucks L.I. in front line. Disposition as per Enemy sent a few shrapnel over LEGEND at 6 p.m. Enemy opened heavily up at FETE ST bombing post at 8.45 p.m. Western nut. Trenches very bad and full to water. Casualties N.C. E.R.	
TRENCHES	30th		A very quiet day and night. A few shells fell in BOYZE TR & WOLF TR. The Bipod Trench Sun was firing every night at gaps in enemy wire, which rendere patrolling impossible. Cas 1 O.R. wounded. E.R.	
"	31st		Front line shrapnelled intermittently during the day. Battalion H.Q. heavily shelled at 6.30 p.m. A small dump with rocket Sig. & VERY LIGHTS was set on fire and partially destroyed. Weather fine and trenches improving though still very wet. Cas 2 O.R. wounded.	

(signed) [signature]
17th R Fusiliers

2nd Division

5th Inf Bde

17th BATTN ROYAL FUSILIERS

SEPTEMBER 1916

Army Form C. 2118.

17 Rly Ins
Sheet 1

WAR DIARY
or
INTELLIGENCE SUMMARY.
(Erase heading not required.)

Instructions regarding War Diaries and Intelligence Summaries are contained in F. S. Regs., Part II. and the Staff Manual respectively. Title pages will be prepared in manuscript.

Place	Date	Hour	Summary of Events and Information	Remarks and references to Appendices
Trenches	Sept 1st		Our front line shelled by shrapnel intermittently during the day about 6.30 pm the vicinity of Batt HQrs was fairly heavily shelled by howitzers a dug knocked in & a store of very lights destroyed & exploded (Cas 1 O.R. wounded	
"	2		A fairly quiet day a little shrapnel burst over our line. At night the enemy fired rifle trench mortars into our front line & did a certain amount of damage to the trench. Our wiring party was out during the night	
"	3		Enemy artillery showed increased activity on our front during the day & night. also minnies & smaller trench mortars. About 5 pm. Batt HQ & Pr was again bombarded with heavy shells. Cas 2 OR killed 3 OR wounded	P.V.A.
"	4		About 5 am a very violent trench bombardment started to the South & increased in intensity for some time. Enemy sent some smoke trench mortar shells also a few minnies, got our rifles into the parapet & started a heavy rapid fire on our bombing post in	S.V.A.
			the evening he was carrying a rifle & 3 bombs	

G. Higgs Col.

Army Form C. 2118

WAR DIARY
or
INTELLIGENCE SUMMARY.

(Erase heading not required.)

Sheet II 1st Royal Fusiliers

Place	Date	Hour	Summary of Events and Information	Remarks and references to Appendices
Trenches	Sept 5		Bn was relieved in the front line. 2 Coys remained in reserve trenches. 1 Coy went to Catincamps. 1 Coy & H.2ts moved to Louvercles in huts. Col. 6.O. wounded	BWD
Reserve	6		Day fine. Our artillery very active during the night	AWB
"	7		Day fine. Enemy shelled Catincamps during the day. 1 man hit on fatigue parade. Cas KOB wounded	AWB
"	8		Training man killed. Day fine	AWB
"	9		Day fine. 2nd anniversary of the formation of the Batt. Band concert & football match in the afternoon	AWB
Trenches	10		Batt relieved 2nd Gr. Baty L.I. in front line. Distribution as before. Enemy active with M.G fire in the evening. We had two men in hole in out. Cas 2nd Lt R C S Gaddum killed	AWB
"	11		Enemy bombarded support line & Batt. H.Qrs heavily for several hours in the afternoon. Our front line suit trench western Batt. H.Qrs damaged. Lt E Robinson 6 R wounded	AWB

M Hope Lt Col

Army Form C. 2118

WAR DIARY
or
INTELLIGENCE SUMMARY.
(Erase heading not required.)

Sheet III

4th Royal Fusiliers

Place	Date	Hour	Summary of Events and Information	Remarks and references to Appendices
TRENCHES	Sept 12		Enemy shelled our flat line + Batt HQ during the day also put a few rifle grenades on our front line about 6 pm. Our artillery carried out a bombardment of intervals during the day. The night was quiet. We had three wounded other ranks.	14th
"	13		We saw + fired upon with Lewis Gun a large enemy working party. Hostile artillery shelled our trenches during the day + put trench mortar into our front line at night. Our Stokes Guns replied. We had [?] wounded other ranks in our trenches. Cas 3 OR wounded.	1AH
"	14		The enemy were very quiet during the day + exhibited a want of [?] at 10.55 pm. We carried a raid out on the enemy trenches in front of our Right Coy. The raiding party consisted of 20 rank + file + 2 officers. They entered the German trench at Zero hours + found it unoccupied. Cas 1 OR slightly wounded. 1AH, 2AH, 3AH	
"	15		A quiet day + night. Very little shelling thrown enemy parties out at night.	1AH
"	16		A day quiet. Batt was relieved in the afternoon + proceeded to COIGNEUX-in-huts	2AH
COIGNEUX	17		" "	1AH
"	18		Very wet	2AH
"	19		Batt evacuated huts + marched to VAUCHELLES-in-huts	3AH

[signature]

Army Form C. 2118

WAR DIARY
or
INTELLIGENCE SUMMARY.
(Erase heading not required.)

Platoon IV 17th Royal Fusiliers

Place	Date	Hour	Summary of Events and Information	Remarks and references to Appendices
VAUCHELLES	Sept 20		En Huts wet day	2AM
"	21		" "	2AM
"	22		Battn. taking part in a liaison demonstration with R.F.C.	2AM
"	23		" " weather fine	2AM
"	24		" "	2AM
"	25		Battn carried out a practice attack on Brigade trenches	2AM
"	26		Fine, under 2 hours notice to move	2AM
"	27		"	2AM
"	28		Weather fine	2AM
"	29		Coy Officers reconnoitred HAMEL VILLAGE line	3AM
"	30		Battn practised night digging	2AM

C.G. Meyer Lt Col
Commanding 17th R Fusiliers

2nd Division.

5th Inf Bde.

17th BATTN   ROYAL FUSILIERS.

OCTOBER 1 9 1 6

Army Form C. 2118.

WAR DIARY
or
INTELLIGENCE SUMMARY.

(Erase heading not required.)

Vol 1 — 17th R Sussex

Instructions regarding War Diaries and Intelligence Summaries are contained in F. S. Regs., Part II. and the Staff Manual respectively. Title pages will be prepared in manuscript.

Place	Date	Hour	Summary of Events and Information	Remarks and references to Appendices
Bruchlett	1-10-16		Attack practice in Brigade trenches	G/A
Bus	2/10/16		Batt. moved into rest of 5th Bde G Bus. Very wet day	G/A
Mailly Maillet	3-		Batt. moved by march to hutment in Mailly Maillet Wood. Very wet	G/A
"	4-		Mailly Maillet Wood	G/A
"	5-			G/A
	6-10-16		Batt. relieved the 1st R. Berk regt. in the trenches Serre Section. Patrols out. A quiet night.	G/A
Serre Sect.	7-10-16		Serre Section Considerable hostile shelling to [?] mortar activity our [?] but no damage. No casualties	G/A
	8-10-16		Serre Section. Hostile shelling in the morning. Our trench mortars [?] active. Batt. relieved by 12th W. Yorks Regt. to afternoon & marched to hutts at Louvencourt	G/A
Louvencourt	9-10-16		In billets	14+
	10-10-16		Batt. took part in Bde practice attack at Divisional trenches	G/A
	11-10-16		Divisional Operations	G/A
	12-10-16		Brigade Operations	G/A

Army Form C. 2118.

WAR DIARY
or
INTELLIGENCE SUMMARY.
(Erase heading not required.)

14th Royal Fusiliers

Place	Date	Hour	Summary of Events and Information	Remarks and references to Appendices
Jean Sillers	13.10.16		Divisional Operations Works in "hulls"	C.J.H
"	14.10.16		Works in "hulls"	C.J.H
"	15.10.16		"	C.J.H
"	16.10.16		Divisional Operations	C.J.H
"	17.10.16		Batt. moved by march into bivouac near Mailly-Maillet. Large working parties supplied by night.	C.J.H
Mailly Maillet	18.10.16		Batt. moved into huts in Mailly Maillet. Mailly Maillet. Batt. supplied large working parties in to trenches	C.J.H
"	19.10.16		"	C.J.H
"	20.10.16		"	C.J.H
"	21.10.16		"	C.J.H
"	22.10.16		Batt. relieved 1st K.R.R's in trenches - Redan Sector. Quiet night - Casualties 1 O.R. killed - 2 O.R. wounded	C.J.H
"	23.10.16		Batt. relieved by 24th R. Fusiliers & 2/H.L.I. in evening. Heavy retaliation to enemy for our bombardment. Casualties 4 O.R. killed & 9 O.R. wounded - marched to huts in Mailly Maillet on relief.	C.J.H
"	24.10.16		In huts in Mailly Maillet	C.J.H

Army Form C. 2118

WAR DIARY
or
INTELLIGENCE SUMMARY.
(Erase heading not required.)

1st Royal Fusiliers

Place	Date	Hour	Summary of Events and Information	Remarks and references to Appendices
Mailly	24.10.16		Billets Mailly Maillet - Very wet	
"	25.10.16		" " - " "	
"	26.10.16		" " - " "	
"	27.10.16		Relieved 2/1st R. Fus. & left hdqrs in Redan Sector. Trouble with a Von Bas state. British Artillery very active. Enemy sent gas - Other patrols out at night. Wire cutting operations taking place.	C.J.H.
			Redan Sector. Artillery active on both sides - Casualties 1 O.R wounded	C.J.H.
	28.10.16		Relieved by 2/R.F. at [?] A.M. and marched to billets in Mailly Maillet	C.J.H.
	29.10.16		Left Mailly Maillet & marched to billets Argoules - Very wet	C.J.H.
	30.10.16			C.J.H.

C.J. Kipper Lt Col
1st (Royal Fusiliers)

2nd Division,

5th Inf Bde.

17th BATTN ROYAL FUSILIERS

NOVEMBER 1916

2nd Division,

5th Inf Bde.

Army Form C. 2118.

WAR DIARY
or
INTELLIGENCE SUMMARY.

(Erase heading not required.)

Vol/3
Nov 1 - Royal Sussex

Place	Date	Hour	Summary of Events and Information	Remarks and references to Appendices
Argoeuves	1-11-16		Battalion in huts at Argoeuves.	Ott
"	2-11-16		" " " "	Ott
"	3-11-16		" " " "	Ott
"	4-11-16		" " " "	Ott
"	5-11-16		" " " "	Ott
"	6-11-16		" " " "	Ott
"	7-11-16		Battalion moved by route march to Acheux Wood - & went into huts in Acheux Wood	Ott
"	8-11-16		" " " "	Ott
"	9-11-16		Battalion moved by route march to Bertrancourt.	Ott
"	10-11-16		Battalion in huts in Bertrancourt - moved to Mailly Wood & on following	Ott
"	11-11-16		All Officers & to N.C.O's made final reconnaissance of forming up position for the forthcoming operations and place bridge in position at 10.15 p.m.	Ott
	12-11-16		Battalion moved from Mailly Wood to their forming up position for the assault. D Sp L Coy - Right front Bn between Clair and Mesnil Trenches with their left on 4th Avenue and their right on 51st Division	Ott

Army Form C. 2118.

WAR DIARY
or
INTELLIGENCE SUMMARY.
(Erase heading not required.)

17th Royal Sussex

Instructions regarding War Diaries and Intelligence Summaries are contained in F.S. Regs., Part II. and the Staff Manual respectively. Title pages will be prepared in manuscript.

Place	Date	Hour	Summary of Events and Information	Remarks and references to Appendices
	12.11.16		Right Support Div. Left front "A" Coy 50 yds West of Charlem Trench with their right on 4th Avenue and their left on 24th Royal Fusiliers. Left Support "C" Coy - Bevr. Hqrs. - Whit Cot.	Ct
Battn. Hd	13.11.16	2.30am	The corps reported in position ready to assault -	Ct
		5.45am	Assault of the German positions north and south of the Ancre started - 2nd Division north of the Ancre with their right on the 51st Division. Beaumont Hamel - 5th Brigade right of the 2nd Division with the left on 6th Bgde. Disposition of 5th Brigade. Right front Battalion 2nd Highland Light Infantry - left front Battalion 24th Royal Fusiliers. Support german 3rd line Septr. 11 Trench (Known as the Green line) Right Support Battalion 17th Royal Fusiliers - Left Support Battalion 2/DCL Bush Light Infr. Objective Munich and Frankfurt Trenches (Known on the Yellow line). Battalion Hd. Qrs. moved up from Whit. to 6 Batn. front line.	Ct
		6.30am	Large numbers of prisoners started to come over	Ct
		9am	Information received that the green line was captured. Bar. Hd. Qrs. moved	Ct

WAR DIARY or INTELLIGENCE SUMMARY

17th Royal Fusiliers

Place	Date	Hour	Summary of Events and Information	Remarks and references to Appendices
	13-11-16	9 a.m.	to Hussar front line and established near Hy 9m.	Ctt
	13-11-16	10 a.m.	Situation at 10 a.m.: Hussar line strongly held by unted men of the S. Bn: from Coys of 17th Royal Fusiliers, extending through 180 men East of Spur dance (count holding centre Lane) and the front nearing S.E. from 26. (Ref 5000 Redan & Pusieux Gpn Sheet). The attack on the left of the S Bn by the VI Bde & further west by the 3rd Division had both failed. Consequently the advance from the Spur down had been held up by enfilade machine gun fire. Small parties of 17th Royal Fusiliers and 2/6th Bde had penetrated into Munich Trench but were unable to maintain themselves in that position.	Ctt
	13-11-16	10.30	JPK reconnoitred the Lewis Gun disposition of Battal & arranged as follows: 2 Companies in Crater Lane from .26 to Wagon Road and two Companies in the front Running from .26 to Southern boundary of Brigade crossing Wagon Road. Blocks and bombing posts established at the junction of Wagon Road. The line was the further east held by our troops north of the Ancre. (Ref 5000 Redan & Pusieux Gpn Sheet)	Ctt

WAR DIARY or INTELLIGENCE SUMMARY

Army Form C. 2118.

17th Royal Fusiliers

Place	Date	Hour	Summary of Events and Information	Remarks and references to Appendices
	13/11/16	1.30pm	Have orders to our Coy to hold the line of the Hedge Row in addition to the two other trenches. Sent up Coys S.A.A. & bombs to coy.	Ott
		4.30pm	Coy reported that they were being counter attacked & that the enemy were working down the front to Beaumont Hamel. Arty. support called for. Attack petered out.	Ott
		5.30pm	Situation quiet	Ott
		12 m/n	Sent up large amount of water and Verey lights to coy.	Ott
	14/11/16		Attack on Munich trench by other batts. did not materialise. Shelled all day. Consolidation continued.	Ott
	15/11/16		Further attack on Munich trench by troops of another Division failed. Position from corp heavily shelled afternoon & evening. Relieved that night and went back to took over night entr-section of Brigade front in old British front line. Casualties.	Ott

Kilton
Haseleton

Army Form C.2118

WAR DIARY
or
INTELLIGENCE SUMMARY.
(Erase heading not required.)

17th Royal Fusiliers

Place	Date	Hour	Summary of Events and Information	Remarks and references to Appendices
	15.11.16		Casualties Killed Wounded Missing Officers - nil Officers 7 Officers nil O.R. 33 O.R. 125 O.R. 22 Total 187 Officers Wounded Lieut E.P. Halloran, 2/Lieuts R.W. Hamilton, G.C. Devere, C.W. Taylor, R. Davison, R. Pearce and H.J. Ricks	
	16.11.16		Battalion in right subsection old British line (Redan Section). Found salvage & burial parties.	
	17.11.16		Battalion relieved at 2.30 pm & marched to billets in Mailly	
	18.11.16		Battalion marched to hutments at Betrancourt	
	19.11.16		Marched as a Brigade to hutments at Arquèves (10 mls)	
	20.11.16		Marched to Candas to billets (12 mls)	
	21.11.16		Marched to St Ouen to billets (5 mls)	

Army Form C. 2118

WAR DIARY
or
INTELLIGENCE SUMMARY.
(Erase heading not required.)

17th Royal Fusiliers

Place	Date	Hour	Summary of Events and Information	Remarks and references to Appendices
	22-11-16		St Ouen - Brigade rested	C.H.
	23-11-16		Marched to Domlyer to billet (10 miles)	C.H.
	24-11-16		Marched to Maison Ponthieu to billet (5 miles)	C.H.
	25-11-16		Marched to Canchy to billet (10 miles)	C.H.
	26-11-16		Canchy - Brigade rested	C.H.
	27-11-16		Marched to Maison Ponthieu. Drafts of 2 men arrived	C.H.
	28-11-16		Marched to Maison Ponthieu (10 miles)	C.H.
	29-11-16		Battalion billeted at Maison Ponthieu	C.H.
	30-11-16			C.H.

(G. Hoppner) Lt Col
17th Royal Fusiliers

2nd Division,
5th Inf Bde.

17th BATTN ROYAL FUSILIERS

DECEMBER 1916

Army Form C. 2118

17th R. Fusiliers

14W

WAR DIARY
or
INTELLIGENCE SUMMARY
(Erase heading not required.)

Instructions regarding War Diaries and Intelligence Summaries are contained in F.S. Regs., Part II. and the Staff Manual respectively. Title Pages will be prepared in manuscript.

Place	Date	Hour	Summary of Events and Information	Remarks and references to Appendices
MAISON PONTHIEU	1/2/16		In billets.	Auth
"	2/2/16		"	Auth
"	3/2/16		"	Auth
"	4/2/16		Companies carrying out programme of work	Auth
"	5/2/16		"	Auth
"	6/2/16		Inspection of Arms close order drill by Brig Gen. Bullen-Smith	Auth
"	7/2/16		Address by G.O.C. 2nd Division	Auth
"	8/2/16		Parade in accordance with programme	Auth
"	9/2/16		Major Jumper assumed command vice Lieut Col Higgins D.S.O. proc'd to 5th Bde.	{2/Lt HARRISON J.G. reported Auth 2/Lt BREDEN E.W.J. for duty } route march for all draft/arrival
"	10/2/16		Tactical exercise by En/Bn Staff at H.L.I. Hd qrs.	2/Lt DYER E.J.R. 2/Lt McHAFFIE W.H. reported for duty. Auth + 80 other ranks
"	11/2/16		Parades as per programme	Auth
"	12/2/16		"	Auth
"	13/2/16		"	Auth
"	14/2/16		"	Firing commenced for all Companies Auth
"	15/2/16		"	Auth
"	16/2/16		"	Auth
"	17/2/16		"	Auth
"	18/2/16		"	Wiring practiced by all Companies Auth

Army Form C. 2118

WAR DIARY
or
INTELLIGENCE SUMMARY
(Erase heading not required.)

Instructions regarding War Diaries and Intelligence Summaries are contained in F. S. Regs., Part II. and the Staff Manual respectively. Title Pages will be prepared in manuscript.

Place	Date	Hour	Summary of Events and Information	Remarks and references to Appendices
MAISON PONTHIEU	19/12/16		In billets. Parade as per programme. Wiring instruction all Companies.	
	20/12/16		" " " " Wiring all Coys.	
	21/12/16		" " " " " "	
	22/12/16		No Parades. Brigade Sports.	
	23/12/16		Instruction in dug out construction, trench digging revetting, all Coys.	
	24/12/16		" "	
	25/12/16		Christmas Day.	
	26/12/16		Parades as per programme. (Dug out construction daily, all (Coys))	
	27/12/16		" " " "	
	28/12/16		" " " " Coy Commanders attended a demonstration of a Platoon exercise under new organisation.	
	29/12/16		" " " "	
	30/12/16		D Coy & half B Coy proceeded to LANNOY & S'tone for Ath.	
	31/12/16		" * C. Coys under Adj. commences work in Reichwood.	

1875 Wt. W593/826 1,000,000 4/15 J.B.C. & A. A.D.S.S./Forms/C. 2118.

2ND DIVISION
5TH INFY BDE

17TH BATTALION

ROYAL FUSILIERS

~~JAN-DEC 1917.~~

1917 JAN — 1918 JAN

To 6 BDE - 2 DIV

5th Brigade.

2nd Division.

17th BATTALION

ROYAL FUSILIERS

JANUARY 1917.

Army Form C. 2118.

WAR DIARY
or
INTELLIGENCE SUMMARY.
(Erase heading not required.)

1st Batt Royal Fusiliers Vol 75

Place	Date	Hour	Summary of Events and Information	Remarks and references to Appendices
MAISON PONTHIEU	1 Jan 1917		In Billets "Zaholiday Regimental Sports. Evening Concert by Band & Minstrel Troupe	
"	2,3,4,5		" Company Programme of Work Carried out	
"	6		"	
"	7		"	
"	8		" Transport unfolded 90 II Corps II Cmdr Shoot in the afternoon	
GEZAINCOURT	9		Left MAISON PONTHIEU marched to GEZAINCOURT weather fine	
"	10		In billets	
VAL DE MAISON	11		Left GEZAINCOURT marched to VAL DE MAISON weather bad under canvas	
RUBEMPRE	12		Left VAL DE MAISON RUBEMPRE Billets	
OVILLERS	13		Left RUBEMPRE in Buses to OVILLERS 2 Coys in OVILLERS Huts 2 Coys in WOLSELEY HUTS	
"	14		In Huts	
"	15			II Cmdr
"	16		B + A OVILLERS and relieved 2nd HLI in Front line A + B Coys front line C + D Coys front 4.30 SAA wounded	
FRONT LINE	17		Weather cold Snow	A + B Lt WEDWARD
"	18		" Front C + D "	+ 2 O.R. wounded
"	19			1 OR
"	20		Relieved by 19th MIDDLESEX " " front marched to BOUZINCOURT arrived 11 AM 21st	
BOUZINCOURT	21		In Billets Divers Front	
"	22		" "	Lt W W EDWARD Died of wounds 21st

Army Form C. 2118.

WAR DIARY
or
INTELLIGENCE SUMMARY.
(Erase heading not required.)

Instructions regarding War Diaries and Intelligence Summaries are contained in F. S. Regs., Part II. and the Staff Manual respectively. Title pages will be prepared in manuscript.

17th Batt Royal Fusiliers

Place	Date	Hour	Summary of Events and Information	Remarks and references to Appendices
Bouzincourt	Jan 23rd 1917		To billets. Snow. Frost continues. 3## 8##	
"	24		" " " " 8##	
"	25		" " " Lt. Col. Cohippins returned from leave and Command 9## 3##	
"	26		" " " "	
"	27		" " " Frost continues 2##	
"	28		Moved to Bruce Huts with 2 other coys 9##	
Bruce Huts	29		In huts. Day & night working parties " " 2##	
"	30		" " " " 3##	
"	31		" " " " 3##	

C.S. Burgoyne
17th Royal Fusiliers

5th Brigade.

2nd Division.

17th BATTALION

ROYAL FUSILIERS

FEBRUARY 1917.

WAR DIARY or INTELLIGENCE SUMMARY.

Army Form C. 2118
Part I
17th Royal Fusiliers

Place	Date	Hour	Summary of Events and Information	Remarks and references to Appendices
OVILLERS		1st	Batt. in BROCE HUTS. Severe Frost. Day and night Working parties. SM	
"		2nd	" " " " " " SM	
"		3rd	" " " " " " SM	
"		4th	" " " " " " Large Bombs dropped SM	
"		5th	near the Huts in the afternoon and at night by aircraft. SM Batt. relieved 1st KRR in the Front Line (COURCELETTE SECTOR) Enemy shelled heavily during the relief. 6 ORs 2 killed 3 wounded SM	
FRONT LINE		6	Some shelling of front line. 6 ORs 1 Killed 1 wounded. SM	
"		7	" " CM	
"		8	" " SM	
"		9	Relieved in the line by 2nd HLI Batt. marched back to WOLFE HUTS SM	
WOLFE HUTS		10	Batt. in Huts. In the evening the Batt. carried out a Raid on the enemy's Front Line Raiding Party consisted of 3.5 ORs and 2nd LT S ANTILL under the command of LT OH IDELSON The operation was entirely successful capturing 4 prisoners and inflicting great loss on the enemy. LT J OELSON wounded 6 ORs wounded 3 ORs Killed 3 missing SM	
"		11	Batt. in Huts. At night a search party was sent out in the hope of finding the missing men - without success. SM	
"		12	Batt. in Huts. Enemy raided our trenches with a party of about town at the same point that we attacked on the 10th but our Lewis gun fire in the Pill Box given by one of the prisoners captured by 17 R. Fusiliers and heavy loss was sustained by the enemy in consequence SM	

Army Form C. 2118

WAR DIARY
Sheet II
INTELLIGENCE SUMMARY
(Erase heading not required.)

14th Royal Fusiliers

Place	Date	Hour	Summary of Events and Information	Remarks and references to Appendices
WOLFE HUTS	Feb 13		Batt'n relieved 2nd H.L.I. in the line 2 Coys in front line 2 Coys in Support dug outs	
FRONT LINE	" 14		Enemy artillery active. 4 O.R. wounded	
"	" 15		Batt'n was relieved by 1st Royal Berks and 1st Kings Regt and marched to billets in BOUZINCOURT	
BOUZINCOURT	" 16		Batt'n moved to OVILLERS HUTS in the evening. Weather much milder	
OVILLERS	" 17		English Attack carried out on 23rd Div front by 6th and 99th Brigades. Batt'n under 2 hours notice to move. Rain and Fog	
BOUZINCOURT	" 18		Marched to BOUZINCOURT in billets	
ALBERT	" 19		Marched to billets in ALBERT	
"	" 20		In billets. Lt JOELSON awarded Military Cross	
"	" 21		"	
"	" 22		"	
"	" 23		" Batt'n marched from ALBERT and relieved 17th MIDDLESEX in Front Line COURCELETTE SECTOR	
FRONT LINE	" 24		Front Line relief complete 1 a.m. 6 O.R., 3 Killed, 5 wounded	
"	" 25		" Enemy discovered to be evacuating his positions. Our front line advanced to new positions	
"	" 26		" Enemy shelled heavily. 3 O.R. wounded 3 O.R. wounded	

Army Form C. 2118.

Sheet VII

WAR DIARY
or
INTELLIGENCE SUMMARY.

(Erase heading not required.)

Place	Date	Hour	Summary of Events and Information	Remarks and references to Appendices
FRONT LINE	Feb	24th	The Battn was relieved in the front line by 2nd Bn Royal Fusiliers and moved to Support dug outs	
Support	"	28	In Support dug outs	2 ORs wounded

C.J. Huggins Lt Col
1st Royal Fusiliers

REPORT on Raid on enemy trench at R.12.c.95.15 and Sap, by 17th Batt.ROYAL FUSILIERS at 8.5 p.m. on 10th Feb.1917.
****

1. The Raiding Party consisted of 2 Officers, 2nd Lieut.JOELSON and 2nd Lieut.ANTILL and 34 other ranks exclusive of covering party and stretcher bearers.

2. The objective embraced the Portion of DESIRE SUPPORT TRENCH for a distance of 200 yards South of the Sap at R.12.c.95.15 and the Sap itself.

3. Previous to the 5th Inst. plans had been got out for a Raid against the enemy's saphead alone without any artillery co-operation, but on taking over the line on the 5th Inst. reconnaissance showed that the enemy's wire had been greatly strengthened at this point and that this plan was no longer feasible.

   On 6th Inst.the final plan was formulated and reconnaissances were carried out on the nights of 6th.,7th.,8th., and 9th.Inst. On the 9th. 2 tapes, one running at right angles to the line of advance and one parallel to the objective to mark the forming up position behind the barrage, were laid out.

3. The following is a description of the Raid:-

   (a). On the night of 9th.Inst. the 17th Royal Fusiliers who had been holding the line, were relieved by the 2/ H.L.I. and came back to WOLFE HUTS.
   (b). On the morning of 10th Inst.a practice over taped lines was held for the Raiding Party.
   (c). At 3 p.m. the whole party paraded and marched to FRASER'S POST where tea was ready for them. Near Battalion Hqrs. rum was issued,white smocks etc. put on and from there the party marched by small groups to the position of assembly between posts 9 & 10.
   By 7.15 p.m. all were in position.
   (d). At 7.55 p.m. the Raiding Party crawled out and got into their position in front of our wire.(Method of advance attached).
   (e). At ZERO.
   Artillery opened intense fire for 3 minutes on objectives and the two parties of Rifle Grenadiers fired into the German Sap.
   During this time the Raiders continued to creep forward.
   (f). At ZERO plus 3 minutes the barrage lifted and rifle grenadier ceased firing. All rushed forward and entered the enemy trench as practised.
   The two blocking parties turned right and left and apparently got into their right positions at approximately points A.& B. on the Map.
   On entering the trench Germans were seen running away to the rear over the parados. Two were shot doing this.
   The left blocking party say, while on the way to their position they killed 6 Germans in a shelter who would'nt come out.
   Both Officers shot two Germans with their revolvers.
   As far as can be gather 4 dug-outs or shaft heads with a fair number of steps, were found and bombed, as the occupants would not be induced to come out
   Seven prisoners (90th Mecklenburghers) were taken. No machine guns were seen.
   No.2 Party under Sgt.Norrington were unable to work their way down the enemy's saphead as our shells were falling in the sap the whole time. They went as far as they could and threw bombs into the Saphead. They think that whatever people were there, must have been killed.
   Lieut.JOELSON stood on the top of the ground at the junction of the Sap with the main trench and directed the affairs. He gave the order to withdraw and stayed himself until the two blocking parties were clear. He was wounded just before the withdrawal.
   (g). No German counter attack was attempted. A certain amount of sniping from the rear of the trench took place.

/.......Some

(g) Continued.

Some bombs were slung from North of the Sap and just as the party was withdrawing a machine gun from somewhere North of the Sap opened.
(h). The enemy put down no barrage. Our intense 3 minutes fire was very effective.

4. Our casualties were 1 Officer and 12 O.R.s. A report as to these will follow later.

5. The following information was obtained regarding the enemy's defences at this point.
(a). WIRE. One row of concertina barbed wire about 3' high. A certain amount of low barbed wire. The men trod it down and had no difficulty in entering the trench.
(b). TRENCHES. About 6' to 7' deep, 3' wide at the bottom, steep sides not revetted. Reported in good order. Not traversed. No continuous fire step. A short fire step near each dug-out entrance. From the trench at intervals, cuttings through the parapet with revetted steps leading towards their wire.
(c). GAS EMPLACEMENTS. No sign of any.
(d). DUG-OUTS. At least 4 entrances were seen and bombed between Sap and our Southern block. Cannot say if they were completed dug-outs. Rather imagine they were shafts with a certain number of steps. Blankets were over entrance door.

----- GENERAL -----

(a). Having tried two methods of artillery co-operation in conjunction with a raid, I prefer the method of starting with an intense fire on the actual objectives to be assaulted by the infantry to the plan of isolating the objective by a box barrage, but leaving the objective itself untouched.
(b). The simple Battalion Code made for the purpose greatly facilitated the transmission and speed of messages.

APPENDIX.

(a). Battalion Orders.
(b). Artillery Programme.
(c). Code.
(d). Formation for advance.
(e). Rough sketch of enemy's trench at objective showing trench not marked on 1/5000 Map.

C.S. Higgins
Lieut.Col.
11/2/17.   Commanding 17th Royal Fusiliers.

SECRET.   BATTALION ORDER NO.17/R/3   9th Feb.1917.
*******   *****************************

1. The Battalion will carry out a raid on the night 10/11 February.

2. Objects of the Raid.
   (a) Kill or capture all enemy encountered.
   (b) Obtain identifications, documents and information as to state of enemy's trenches.
   (c) Capture or destroy any enemy machine guns or Trench mortars found.
   (d) Bomb dugouts and inflict generally maximum of loss on enemy.

3. The objective will be that portion of DESIRE SUPPORT TRENCH for a distance of 200 yards South of Sap at R.12.c.95.15 and the latter Sap.

4. The Raiding force will be under the command of Lieut. JOELSON and will be divided into 3 parties composed and armed as follows:-
   No.1 PARTY.
   2nd Lieut. ANTILL) 3 men carry revolvers and bludgeons, Remainder Rifle
   16 O.Ranks.   ) and bayonet. All men 2 bombs in pockets, 2 men for
) each stop an extra 12 bombs each in bucket.

   No.2 PARTY.
   Sgt. Norrington) 1 man revolver and bludgeon, remainder rifle and
   6 O.Ranks.   ) bayonet. All to carry 2 bombs in pockets and 1 man
) an extra 12 bombs in bucket.

   No.3 PARTY.
   Lieut. JOELSON.) 2 men revolver and bludgeon, remainder rifle and
   10 O.Ranks.   ) bayonet, all to carry 2 bombs in pocket
) and 2 men to carry 12 bombs each in bucket
) in addition.

   Rifles will be loaded with 10 rounds and 1 spare clip carried in breast pocket. All men will carry wire cutters. Equipment will not be worn.
   A covering party of 2 Lewis Guns and teams and 4 Rifle grenadiers will remain in the British line and be disposed as follows:-
      1 Lewis Gun between Posts No.9 & 10.
      1   "   "   "   "   " 10 & 11.
      4 Rifle Grenadiers at Post 10.
      4   "   "   in trench between Posts 9 & 10.

5. The Raiding Force will assemble in the trench between Posts No.9 and No.10.
   They will be in position ready to move by 7.30 p.m.

6. Action of parties at ZERO.
   (a) At ZERO our artillery will open 3 minutes intense fire on enemy's front line trench from M.13.b.7.7. to R.12.c.6.7.
   (b) Immediately fire opens parties will crawl out from their assembly positions and get as close up to the barrage as possible on a front of 30 yards.
   Parties will move out in the following order No.1, No.2, No.3 Party.
   There will be a distance of 20 yards between parties.
   The right hand man of No.2 Party will be immediately in rear of the left hand man of No.1 Party.
   The left of No.1 Party will direct and will move on a bearing of 65°
   (Magnetic)

6a. COVERING PARTY.
    Immediately the artillery opens fire at ZERO the 4 Rifle Grenadiers at Post 10 will fire at the enemy's sentry at the saphead. The 4 Grenadiers between No.9 & 10 Posts will fire at the suspected M.G. Emplacement near the junction of Sap and main trench. The two Lewis Guns will not fire except for the purpose of covering the withdrawal of the raiding party and preventing any of the enemy working round the flanks of the party during their withdrawal.

7. At ZERO plus 3 minutes artillery will lift off objectives of raiding
   /...........parties

Sheet 2.

parties and all parties will move forward and enter enemy's trench and act as follows:-

No.1 PARTY will ~~followxxxxx~~ enter the enemy's trench by the gap in the wire just South of the Sap and place stops of 4 bombers each at points marked A & B on the Map. Remainder of this party will deal with any dugouts, machine guns and enemy met with.

No.2 Party, will follow No.1, turn left before reaching enemy's main trench and enter enemy's Sap close to its junction with main trench and deal with enemy post there.

No.3 Party, will follow No.2 and enter enemy's trench at the same point as No.1.-This party will act as reinforcement to either No.1 or No.2 Parties and will go to wherever most opposition is being met with. All parties are to use rifle & bayonet as far as possible for dealing with the enemy. Bombs are not to be thrown into the trench before jumping in.

8. The method of withdrawal will be issued as a separate order.

9. (a) 4 Stretcher bearers with 2 stretchers will follow 50 yards in rear of No.3 party. They will take cover in shell holes close to the enemy's wire sending one man forward to keep in touch with raiding force in enemy's trench.
(b) One stretcher and 4 bearers will remain at each of Posts No.9 & 10.
(c) 2 stretchers and 8 bearers in reserve at Advd.Battn.Hqrs..
Wounded stretcher cases will be carried as far as possible to No.9 Post. Any coming in at any other post will be taken by the trench to No.9 Post from whence the M.O. will arrange for their evacuation via the East Boundary track.

10. Telephone communication.
Telephone communication will be established from the position of assembly to both Coy.Hqrs. at Posts 14 & 9. A line will also be laid from Post 9 to Post 8 (Hqrs.of left Coy.of right Battalion).

11. Lieut.SKEAD, 3 runners and 2 telephone operators will remain at the telephone at the position of assembly. He will have a complete roll of the raiding force and check them on return and will inform stretcher bearers of any missing.
He will inform Advd.Batt.Hqrs. as to the situation as early as possible by telephone or runner if line broken.

12. Prisoners and captured documents will be sent direct to Advd. Batt.Hqrs.under escort. Two men per 10 prisoners should be sufficient. If the enemy's barrage is down they will wait on our front line until situation becomes quiet.

13. Gaps thro' our wire will be cut on the night 9/10th by a reconnoitring party under Lieut.JOELSON'S orders.

14. All identifications, papers etc.will be taken from the raiding party before leaving WOLFE HUTS.

15. All ranks will be warned that in the event of capture they are only to disclose their rank, name and number.

16. Every man of the raiding force will wear white overalls, white helmet covers and white rifle and bludgeon covers.
Boots and men's faces will be chalked.

17. Advanced Batt.Hqrs at W.Miraumont Road.
18. Artillery programme attached.
19. ZERO hour will be communicated later.
20. Watches will be synchronised from 5th Bde.Hqrs. at 12 noon and 4 p.m. on the 10th February.

SECRET.

AFTER ORDER
to
BATTALION ORDER No.17/R/3 d/-9/2/17.

METHOD OF WITHDRAWAL. Lieut.JOELSON or senior officer or N.C.O. will station himself at the junction of Sap with main trench. All parties immediately on completion of their task will send a man to report to him there.

When he judges the time favourable he will sound the horn which will be the signal for everyone to withdraw except the two blocking parties who will remain at their posts.

The second blast on the horn will be the signal for the blocks to withdraw who will cover the retirement of the remainder.

All parties will withdraw by the same gap as they entered by unless word has reached them that the wire round the saphead has been cleared.

All men will report to Lieut.SKEAD in the trench between No.9 & 10 Posts. If they get back by any other route they must work their way along the trench until they find him.

10/2/17.

CODE for 10.2.17.

GERTIE,,,,,,,,,,,Raiding force have entered enemy's trenches.
DOROTHY..........Prisoners are coming in.
Mabel............Raiding force cannot get through enemy's wire.
ETHEL............Raiding force repelled by enemy.
PHYLLIS..........Believe raid entirely sucessful.
TEDDY............Believe raid has failed.
MAUDE............Send up reserve stretchers.
CONSTANCE........All raiders have returned.
FLO 4 ....4 raiders still to come in.

ARTILLERY PROGRAMME.

(a) At ZERO intensive fire will be opened from M.13.b.7.7; to R.12.c.8.7.

(b) At ZERO plus 3 minutes artillery barrage between M.13.b.3.9 and and M.7.d.0.4. will lift and fall on the PYS ROAD as far as posts at xxxxxxxxxx M.7.d.6.5. thence to trench at M.7.d.2.7 down the trench to M.7.d.0.5.

(c) At ZERO plus 18 minutes rate of artillery will be reduced.

(d) At ZERO plus 60 minutes artillery fire will cease.
The right group will fire a box barrage as a feint starting at ZERO and continuing to ZERO plus 20 minutes on the German front line at M.8.d.6.0.

D

Formation for Advance

←——— 30ˣ ———→

| Left Block Bombers | Bayonet Men | Right Block Bombers |

No 1 Party

Support Bayonet Men

✕ 2/Lt Antill

Two Bombers
Four Bayonet Men

No 2 Party

↕ 20ˣ

✕ Lt Joelson

No 3 Party

BRIEF SUMMARY OF INFORMATION REGARDING RAID
on night 10/11th FEBY. 17.

GS 740/84

Our raiding party had no difficulty in getting out under cover of our Artillery Barrage. AT Zero + 5 minutes they entered enemy's trench. Hostile wire proved no obstacle and no opposition was encountered.

A number of Germans were seen running away from the enemy's front line and bombs were thrown after them, rifle shots were also fired at them - no definite report yet as to whether any casualties were inflicted on these Germans. At least five dugouts were seen in the portion of the front line raided. As the enemy could not be induced to come out of these dugouts they were bombed with Mills and M S K hand granades and rifle shots were also fired down them.

In, ar least, two cases groans were heard inside the dugouts and it is believed that several casualties were inflicted in this way.

Seven prisoners were captured alive, these men offered no resistance and appeared very glad to be taken prisoner. All prisoners captured belonged to the 90th MECKLENBURG Regoment.

Enemy's barrage was not intense and merely consisted of desultory shelling from 8 p.m. to 8.30 p.m.

A full report will be rendered as soon as O.C. 17th Royal Fusiliers has had time to collect the required information.

Casualties ascertained up to date.

Captain S. JOELSON wounded, 1 other rank killed, 5 other ranks wounded of whom 2 were only slight cases.
There are also four missing, but these are believed to have returned safely to our line and will probably rejoin their regiment during the night.

1 a.m.
11/2/17.

Brigadier General,
Commanding, 5th Infantry Brigade.

1038/OM/40
B.G.12

2nd Division

I forward herewith report from O.C.
17 Royal Fusiliers as to the steps taken
to recover the men missing from the raid on
10th inst.

G.M. Walterkite B.G
13.2.17.   Comdg. 5th Inf. Bde

Attach to copy
of O/C of Raid

No further action

Secret.

2nd Division

With reference to the raid last night, I regret that I am unable to forward the full report tonight, as I had hoped.

O.C. 17th Royal Fusiliers has written to me that he has been engaged all day in sifting men's statements, and he is sending up a party tonight to make a further search for the 5 men reported missing.

From what he has been able to find out, I fear most of our casualties were caused by guns continuing to fire on the sap up to zero + 3 minutes. I have seen ~~Brigadier~~ Brig. Lt. Col. Dormer about this, also the Battery commander whose guns were on this point. They are both enquiring into the matter, but I have not yet heard from them.

As regards the casualties they are now reported to be as under.

    Killed   1 O.R.
    Wounded   Lieut. Jackson and 6 O.R.
    Missing   5 O.R.

Also 1 officer and 1 O.R. 2/ H.L.I. were slightly wounded.

As regards the missing men, both the officers of the raiding party say that they are sure none of our men were left in the enemy's trenches, but no one, including the stretcher bearers who were out after the raiding party had returned, saw more than the one man killed.

O.C. 17th Royal Fusiliers informs me that 6 Germans were killed in a shelter by his left blocking party, and several dugouts bombed with Mills and P.C.R. bombs.

I will forward his report directly it is received.

G. M. Hutchison B.G.
Comdg. 5 Inf. Bde.

11.2.17

5th Bde.

1038/OP/40

The casualties in raid of 10/11th are now proved to be as follows:-

Killed
2 O.R.

Wounded
1 Officer
6 O.R.

Missing
4

Total 13

I regret that these men are missing & that no proof or trace of any kind of what has happened to them can be brought forward. Both the officers and the right and left blocking parties who were the last to leave the trench are positive that none of our men were left there.

A thorough search of "No Man's Land" was made the night of 10/11th & yesterday an officer's party went all over the ground for several hours without finding more than the two dead men.

Of course, bodies wrapped

on them. White overalls are extremely difficult to locate in the snow.

The remarkable thing is that not a single man in the raiding party can throw the slightest light on what might have happened to them.

No one appears to have heard any one of these men cry out or seen them fall or know anything about them. Three of the missing belonged to the small party of 6 under Sgt Norrington whose mission was to capture the Saphead. This party only succeeded in getting a few yards down the Sap owing to our artillery fire & returned via the main trench. So must have seen the men if they were killed in the trench. This apparently must have been killed in No Man's Land.

I fear that nothing more will be heard of these men.

C.S. Higgins Lt Col
17th Royal Fusiliers

12.2.17

5th Brigade.

2nd Division.

17th BATTALION

ROYAL FUSILIERS

M A R C H   1917.

Army Form C. 2118

WAR DIARY or INTELLIGENCE SUMMARY

SHEET 1 17th Batt. ROYAL FUSILIERS 5/2

(Erase heading not required.)

Place	Date	Hour	Summary of Events and Information	Remarks and references to Appendices
COURCELETTE	March 1st		Battalion in support 2 Coys COURCELETTE dug outs 2 Coys CHALK MOUNDS Day & night Working Parties	
			MAJOR R. TURNER assumed command of 6th NORTHANTS REGT	
	2		Battalion in support " " " " "	
	3		" " relieved by 22nd Royal Fusiliers Marched to billets in ALBERT Baths	
ALBERT	4		Batt. HQrs WOLFE HUTS Companies in Billets at ALBERT	
	5		" Companies detached on working parties	
	6		" " " "	
	7		" " " "	
	8		" " " "	
	9		" " " Snow	
	10		" " " "	
OVILLERS HUTS	11		Batt. moved to OVILLERS HUTS Working parties provided	
	12		" in huts " " "	
	13		" " " " "	
	14		" " " " "	
COURCELETTE	15		Batt. moved to COURCELETTE and Hatchet Camp Working parties	
	16		" in tents Working Parties CAPT A HOWARD wounded	
	17			

Army Form C. 2118

WAR DIARY
or
INTELLIGENCE SUMMARY

(Erase heading not required.)

SHEET II 17th Batt. ROYAL FUSILIERS

Place	Date	Hour	Summary of Events and Information	Remarks and references to Appendices
COURCELETTE	March 18th 1917		Battalion in Tents Working Parties	
"	" 19		" " " "	
OVILLERS HUTS	" 20		" " Huts " " (Battn marched to OVILLERS HUTS in the afternoon)	
"	" 21		" " " "	
HEDAUVILLE	" 22		Marched to HEDAUVILLE	
"	" 23		In Billets	
"	" 24		" " Lt Col R.G. HIGGINS assumed Command 5th July Bn CAPT S.J.M. HOLE in Command of Battalion	
RUBEMPRE	" 25		Marched to RUBEMPRE	
"	" 26		In Billets	
GEZAINCOURT	" 27		Marched to GEZAINCOURT CAPT L.M. GLASSON in command of Battn	
NUNCQ	" 28		" " NUNCQ	
CROIX	" 29		" " CROIX	
"	" 30		In Billets	
PERNES	" 31		Marched to PERNES In Billets Training commenced cold and wet	

C.J. Higgins
L.Col
17. Royal Fusiliers

5th Brigade.
2nd Division.

17th BATTALION

ROYAL FUSILIERS

APRIL 1917.

WAR DIARY
of the 1/4th or Royal Fusiliers
INTELLIGENCE SUMMARY.

March ~~April 1917~~

Army Form C. 2118
Vol 18
5/2

Place	Date	Hour	Summary of Events and Information	Remarks and references to Appendices
PERNES	1st to 3rd		The regiment was in billets having marched from CROIX. Men's billets had with cleanly roofs. Training took the form of lectures to officers and ample details of stamps that often warned which we were required would be in full swing shortly. An inspection and rehearsal of guard procedure was carried out by companies and mark the lighting that disposed of on the way to and from the actual operations.	
"	4th		Major R.J. BRETT, 2/Oxf. and Bucks. L. Infy. took over the duties of officer i/c - 46. ino. of from Major R. TURNER. Step was two appointed to command 1st 6/Northamptonshire Regiment.	
"	6th		(Good Friday). Training suspended to enable men to attend church.	
"	7th		Orders received to prepare to be in line near BOURIE. Men batted, clean washing issued.	

WAR DIARY
or
INTELLIGENCE SUMMARY.
(Erase heading not required.)

Army Form C. 2118

Place	Date	Hour	Summary of Events and Information	Remarks and references to Appendices
PERNES	8th		Voluntary church in the morning. Regiment paraded at 3pm to march to PREVILLERS (3 miles). About 12 men fell out and rejoined later. Billets good. Fine day.	
PREVILLERS	9th		Snowed heavily. Men rested and bathed. Football match.	
MAROEUIL	10th		Horsed to MAROEUIL in heavy snow-storms. Day of big attack on whole army front. Gained German front line from VIMY to CROISILLES. Billeted in broken down houses. Men marched well.	
In line	11th		Relieved 51st Brigade after their successful attack and moved into reserve line (old British front line) 500 yds north of ROCLINCOURT. Blinding snow storm.	
In line	12th		Spent morning in clearing up battlefield. Buried corpses and established salvage dump. Moved up in the evening to the Blue (or Red German support) line, relieving the York & Lancs Regt. Left 40 men in support of the 2/4 R.F.	

A5834 Wt. W4973/M687 750,000 8/16 D. D. & L. Ltd. Forms/C.2118/13.

WAR DIARY or INTELLIGENCE SUMMARY

Army Form C. 2118

Place	Date	Hour	Summary of Events and Information	Remarks and references to Appendices
In the line	13th		In German support line, carrying party sent to 2nd Royal Fusiliers at SUGAR FACTORY. One of the first victims (Simpkin) died of concussion from view, seems to have been forgotten. The party walked on the sky-line near B BILLEV in close formation, the German started shelling and upset Fatigue. 1 was killed, unfortunately it was the third and last kill to our own sw.	
	14th		Moved to the BROWN, or German reserve line, connecting up with the 1st Canadian Division on the left and the Naval Division on the right. Headquarters and one company in TOMMY TRENCH. Trenches shelled but few casualties.	sw
	15th		Moved to Front line (so-called) which consisted of a few posts on either side of the ARRAS-OPPLEUX road, and about 1000 yards from the OPPY line. This was a sunken lane from the main HINDENBURG line. Posts were shelled heavy during the night under heavy shell-fire. Two companies were in the support line 500 yards behind the posts.	sw

WAR DIARY
or
INTELLIGENCE SUMMARY.
(Erase heading not required.)

Army Form C. 2118

Place	Date	Hour	Summary of Events and Information	Remarks and references to Appendices
In the line	16th		1st Lts. posts and support line. Daylight reconnaissance of OPPY line and ARLEUX switch ordered by Brigade. Lieut BRODIE and 3 men moved out about 3 p.m. line obviously held. Party sniped from ARLEUX. Lieut BRODIE wounded and prisoner; Cpl TOWN killed; one man wounded and prisoner; one man got back safe. This amounts to show that a day light reconnaissance of a prepared line is not desirable in day light. Wire was thick and unbroken.	S.A.
"	17th		Battalion ordered to find 3 companies to enter ARLEUX SWITCH and bomb from left to right in conjunction with 9th R. Fus. Letts on the right. Brigade was informed that wire was unbroken and division stopped the attack. On its subsequently happening this was very fortunate as our separate supports in turn failed to take the line. Heavy shelling; 1 man killed and 2 wounded (Acoy). See O.O. No 10.	S.A.
"	18th		The regiment moved back to the old Reserve trench near ECURIE having been relieved by the 13th Essex Regt.	S.A.

A3834 Wt. W4973/M687 750,000 8/16 D.D. & L. Ltd. Forms/C.2118/13.

WAR DIARY
or
INTELLIGENCE SUMMARY.
(Erase heading not required.)

Army Form C. 2118.

Place	Date	Hour	Summary of Events and Information	Remarks and references to Appendices
hit the line	19th		Trench book repaired and exchanged, and a clean change of washing to men could be done owing to Officers and men alike being in dug-out and trenches in trenches.	—
"	20th		Lt. Col. C.P. Higgins D.S.O. left the regiment to command the 114th Brigade. Lieut. Col. S.V.P. Weston assumed command of the regiment from second in command 1/Bn. a(Ratcliffe returned. Still in Dal Rublik line "resting".	—
"	21st		Moved to Quarry reserve line (BROWN)	—
"	22nd		Moved to railway from B.15 c 7.0 to B.8 9 6 (1:40,000) the regiment started to dig a main line of defence 150 yards front of this line. Every man dug to accommodate one company which then occupied the line. The other three companies dug a way west of the railway.	—
"	23rd		to line of trek ham line of defence further improved by A & D coys. intermittent shelling of portions front of line.	—

WAR DIARY
or
INTELLIGENCE SUMMARY.
(Erase heading not required.)

Army Form C. 2118.

Place	Date	Hour	Summary of Events and Information	Remarks and references to Appendices
	24th		Still on railway line. Bn. line of defence firmed up and linked to that made by Canadians on left and 99th Bigde on the right. Shelling heavy during day.	
	25th		Moved back to BROWN line and TOMMY TRENCH. Orders received to attack ORPY line and WILLOW SWITCH on a date to be notified later.	
	26th		Day chiefly spent in equipping & fitting for the hunt.	
	27th		Moved up to battle positions. See O.O. 11. A few casualties near the tunnel and later in tommy sap position.	
	28th	4.25 am	Regiment, after it ran into strong bomb & carrying parties, & snipers etc., and attacked the 2/H.L.I. and 2/Stafford Regts. going over. Canadian on the left panic. Arleux and 2/94th Bush Light took their line objective, but to be 2/94th were very badly harassed & it succeeded ended. The 2/H.L.I. were very badly harassed & it 6.x. Brigade were driven back to their original line, the 63rd division on the right side did not advance.	

WAR DIARY
or
INTELLIGENCE SUMMARY

Army Form C. 2118.

Place	Date	Hour	Summary of Events and Information	Remarks and references to Appendices
			Leave Stair Kermal. B Coy, attached to 7/4th formed the right of the Brigade in an Cabken 74x202 thereupon formed a defensive flank. As all an officer had not been carried for out of the trenches, prob were not of a job; they eventually established posts on the German front line. The Carrying parties did six journeys that day, and the methods up went later to stiffen up the line. An enemy sniper - a black that "held" two M.G. redts evinced a certain amount of "panic" and as evinced by frequent S.O.S. signals. Shelling.	GRU
	29th		Huns got down to an old line and then left front line. Very heavy shelling all day and night. Orders received that the regiment, the 9/4th, the 9/4 R.F. and the ? would continue to hold the line while the 12 R.F. and the 9.42 Brigade would again attack OPPY village and wood.	GRU

Instructions regarding War Diaries and Intelligence Summaries are contained in F. S. Regs., Part II. and the Staff Manual respectively. Title pages will be prepared in manuscript.

WAR DIARY
or
INTELLIGENCE SUMMARY.
(Erase heading not required.)

Army Form C. 2118.

Place	Date	Hour	Summary of Events and Information	Remarks and references to Appendices
	30th	3.45am	Attack commenced. Result; 24th R F gained their first objective but 99th Brigade could make no headway, and both had to retire on to their original line. As a result of the operations the regiment was highly praised by the other regiments of the brigade for the part it had played and the way in which it had helped them. A list of recommendations is shown as under:-	
			Military Cross:- a/Captain F.L. Taylor; 2/Lieut H.A. Panting; 2/Lieut A. Forbes-Menzies; 2/Lieut H.S. Havelock.	
			D.C.M. Sergeant H. Thorn (B coy)	
			Mil. Medal. L/C A.J.R. Sinclair. L/C E. Perkins. L/C W. A.H. Wood; L/C S.J.H. Mudd. Pte A.E. Coppock.	
			Casualties: 111 all ranks.	
			Names of Officers 2/Lt E.J. BEITLE killed 28/4/17; 2/Lt S. SHEPPARD " 28/4/17; 2/Lt A. FORBES MENZIES wounded 28/4; 2/Lt E.W. BRATCHEL "; 2/Lt R.L. BATEMAN " 30/4/17; 2/Lt H.G. HECKLE 3/5/17	S.R. [illegible] Lt Col Commanding 24th Royal Fusiliers

A5834 Wt. W4973/M687 750,000 8/16 D. D. & L. Ltd. Forms/C.2118/13.

5th Brigade.
2nd Division.

17th BATTALION

ROYAL FUSILIERS

MAY 1917

WAR DIARY
or
INTELLIGENCE SUMMARY.

1/4th Royal Fusiliers

Army Form C. 2118

MAY — MAY — MAY

Place.	Date	Hour	Summary of Events and Information	Remarks and references to Appendices
KLEEMAN STELLUNG TRENCH	1-3		Battalion Hqrs., 23 officers and 96 other ranks were ordered to form a composite company on this Ist (?) under Lt. Col. N.J.P. WESTON DSO MC. This composite company formed from the 6th and 99th Brigades under Brigadier General KELLETT were given the task of capturing OPPY WOOD and VILLAGE. The composite company was in reserve and not used, the attack having failed to obtain its objective. The remainder of the battalion under Major R.T. BRETT returned to TOMMY TRENCH and the KLEEMAN STELLUNG on the night 8/10 1/2nd and at 2 pm on 10th 2nd were ordered to form up on the LENS-ARRAS road and march to X huts ECOIVRES. The battalion less composite company, arrived in camp at 6.30 pm. On the 3rd battalion was made and the day was spent in rest and washing.	
ECOIVRES	4		The battalion less composite company marched to CAMBLIGNEUL and went up to hills for the night. No casualties on the march on skills B head and about Lieut-Col Weston joined the battalion having been and the composite company joined the battalion having been conveyed from ST CATHERINE'S in motor lorries.	
CAMBLIGNEUL				

WAR DIARY
INTELLIGENCE SUMMARY

Army Form C. 2118.

MAY 1918

Place	Date	Hour	Summary of Events and Information	Remarks and references to Appendices
DIEVAL	5		Marched to DIEVAL (11 miles) and went into good billets there. Two men fell out on the last mile, and this was chiefly due to the unusual heat.	
DIEVAL	6-16		This period was spent in reorganization and training. The strength of the Battalion was further reduced to an average return strength of 532 all ranks, and it became necessary to reorganize companies into two Platoons each of two sections:- 2 Lewis Gun sections, 1 bombing section, 1 rifle grenade section and 1 section of riflemen. 2 Officers and 23 other ranks arrived from RUYRER on the 6th, but apart from these and a few odd sick men no drafts of any strength were received. The training had the following forms:- (1) Arms and Squad drill (2) Lewis Gun. Mechanism and stoppages firing on range by every member. (3) Bombing with dummies first and live afterwards. (4) Bayonet fighting. (5) Musketry. Rapid loading, aiming, Trench exercises, battle firing on range. (6) Gas drill.	

WAR DIARY
INTELLIGENCE SUMMARY.

17th Royal Fusiliers

MAY

Army Form C. 2118.

Place	Date	Hour	Summary of Events and Information	Remarks and references to Appendices
DIEVAL			(4) Rifle meets drill, including team shoot rifle. This latter fires a bomb nearly 100 yards further than the ordinary rifle. (5). Firing. Team of 6 men on 15 short shakes, barked arms and concertina. (6). Regimental "money" schemes for signallers under S/Sergt HART. In addition there was a bombing class under Sergt YOUNG, a topography class for officers and N.C.O.'s under Captain GREENWOOD and a sniping class under their M/HARRIS. An inspection of the transport was held by the Q.M. & O.C. and showed the report them as follows:- "Harness good but not so good as S/M.Q.C. vehicles excellent, one shortage of greate observed." The commanding officer inspected A and C coys on the 15th, and B and D coys on the 16th. 5. Their MIDDLEY (Canadian etc.) and ENGLAND (drummer etc.) were very helpful, a court-martial presided over by Brigadier-General Walsh and were found guilty. Various XX football matches were played probably.	

WAR DIARY
or
INTELLIGENCE SUMMARY
17th ROYAL FUSILIERS

MAY

Army Form C. 2118.

Place	Date	Hour	Summary of Events and Information	Remarks and references to Appendices
DIEVAL	6-16		Off cers v. Sergeants. 3-0 17th R.F. v. H.L.I. 0-1 Off cers v. Officers H.L.I. 6-1 Company Tournament. A Final 1-0 winning team received 55 francs. A dry and wet canteen were opened, and proved a great success, showing a 10% profit on sales. Voluntary services were held each Sunday.	
ECOIVRES	17		The regiment marched back to huts and tents in ECOIVRES (14 miles); no casualties. 3 Officers, 1 W.O., & 8 NCO's went to PERNES for the training of drafts.	
HULL CAMP	18		Marched to HULL CAMP, 9.10 G, E of LENS — Arrival load. tents and bivouacs. Working party (2 coys) went on early and day till 2.30 p.m. under R.E. supervision of 96 & 6.4. Football match for those in camp v. H.L.I.	

A5834 Wt.W4973/M687 750,000 8/16 D.D. & L. Ltd. Forms/C.2118/13.

Army Form C. 2118.

WAR DIARY
or
INTELLIGENCE SUMMARY.
(Erase heading not required.)

1/4 [illegible] MAY 1917

Instructions regarding War Diaries and Intelligence Summaries are contained in F.S. Regs., Part II. and the Staff Manual respectively. Title pages will be prepared in manuscript.

Place	Date	Hour	Summary of Events and Information	Remarks and references to Appendices
HULL CAMP	19-23		The regiment found 160 men each day for road-making etc on the Maison de la Cote Road. Complete units were taken including their own companies. The remaining companies in camp underwent training and special attention was paid to the new Lewis guns & rifle Grenades. Rifle practices were carried on V. On the nights of the 23rd four officers went to the line to be attached to the 1/Bedfords, 54th division, un til the regiment took over.	
In the line	24th		The regiment took over L.4. (HALLEUX) sector from 1/Bedfords, having the Canadians on the left and the 2/4/4 on the right. B coy was on the left and C coy on the right. The front line in front (East) of ARLEUX - HELGIN, A + B coys were in the support trench (original ARLEUX LOOP). During the relief reg/s BECK and CORPORAL WILSHAM [?] were [illegible]	

WAR DIARY
INTELLIGENCE SUMMARY

Army Form C. 2118.

Month: May 17th

Place	Date	Hour	Summary of Events and Information	Remarks and references to Appendices
In the line	25		were killed and 8 other ranks were wounded. Intermittent shelling of front line during the day. Battalion HQrs also marked down. During the night communicating with the Canadians was re-established on the left. The front line trench being joined up. Patrols under 2/Lieut Mead and Campbell found German consolidating their position in front of FRESNOY PARK (about 600 yards from our position).	
"	26		Day quiet. Patrols went out at night under 2/Lieut Aycough and 2/Lt England. A listening post was established on the FRESNOY road, and a rifle post at the junction of our front line and the communicating trench to the German trenches. The front line was very heavily shelled between 1 and 2am on the night 26/27.	
"	27		Day quiet. At about 10 pm we shelled enemy ration dumps with our	

WAR DIARY
INTELLIGENCE SUMMARY.

Army Form C. 2118.

Month: May 17th [Hooge Sector?] field

Place	Date	Hour	Summary of Events and Information	Remarks and references to Appendices
In the field	27		Gas and lachrymatory. There was no retaliation. Patrols went out under officers Rysbergh and Sheat to approach PARK. The enemy's bnd was not wired and very little work was apparent. The south end was considerable stronger. At about 1am the Canadians on our left were raided: no enemy reached their trenches. 2 Kink Doncaster and Eastbourne [formed?] for shelby.	
	28		Very heavy shelling during the May day: 1 man killed and 2 sent down suffering from shell-shock. The afternoon was relieved by 2/4th R.F. at about 10 mn, and went back to the reserve line about EMROS Wood. The enemy retaliated for shelling of nakin dumps.	
	29-31		Intermittent shelling of EMROS area.	

Army Form C. 2118.

WAR DIARY
or
INTELLIGENCE SUMMARY.
(Erase heading not required.)

May 1st, 1917. [illegible]

Place	Date	Hour	Summary of Events and Information	Remarks and references to Appendices
In the line	31		Relieved 24th Royal Fusiliers on the night of 31/1 in the ARLEUX LOOP (L4) sector. Serjt Beck and Pamick and Cpl Wilhowie R.A.M.C. killed by a shell on enemy barrage where it crosses WILLERVAL road. No further casualties.	Cas.
	3/5/17		[signed] CH Winter Lieut-Col. Comdg 17th Royal Fusiliers	

5th Brigade.

2nd Division.

17th BATTALION

ROYAL FUSILIERS

JUNE 1917

Army Form C. 2118.

WAR DIARY
14th Royal Fusiliers
INTELLIGENCE SUMMARY
June

Place	Date	Hour	Summary of Events and Information	Remarks and references to Appendices
ARLEUX en GOHELLE	1/6/17		The Battalion completes its final three days in front line without incident.	S/Rs
HULL Camp	3/6/17		Relieved by 17th Middlesex and marched to transport lines where bus served. Later to Anzin St Aubin.	S/Rs
ANZIN ST AUBIN	4/6/17 to 10/6/17		Working parties daily to front line and back areas. All ranks through the 9 as a member at ECURIE. Swimming races held in the local stream. Lt Col S.V.P. WESTON to G.H.Q. conference at Boulogne. Major R. BRETT assumes command.	S/Rs
Railway Embankment BAILLEUL	11/6/17 to 13/6/17		The Battalion in support to the Brigade. Usual nightly working parties. Very quiet.	S/Rs
BUDBROOKS Camp	14/6/17		All ranks put into shorts. Work, making overland track from ROCLINCOURT to front line.	S/Rs

20h

Army Form C. 2118.

WAR DIARY
or
INTELLIGENCE SUMMARY.
(Erase heading not required.)

14th _____ June _____

Instructions regarding War Diaries and Intelligence Summaries are contained in F.S. Regs., Part II. and the Staff Manual respectively. Title pages will be prepared in manuscript.

Place	Date	Hour	Summary of Events and Information	Remarks and references to Appendices
BUDBROOKE CAMP	17/6/17		No 21 Sgt THORN. H. awarded the D.C.M. This gallant N.C.O., wounded 2/6/17 has been through all engagements with battalion since its arrival in FRANCE and has been three times recommended.	SNS
MONT St ELOY.	19/6/17		Billeted in the outhouses of the monastery. XIII Corps Horse Show.	SNS
BETHUNE	29/6/17		Arrived here by 'bus. Billeted in the Orphanage.	SNS
Canal Left	2/6/17		Took over from 2/10 MANCHESTER Regiment. Very good handing over. This sector of trenches in which the battalion received its baptism of fire was held first in November 1915. Very quiet.	SNS
	28/6/17	9 pm	Heavy trench mortar and light gun bombardment for two hours on left company and KINGS on our left. After which the Germans raided RED DRAGON crater - in reality part of trench the Battalion front - CSM. MINES killed. No change.	SNS
	30/6/17			

5th Brigade
2nd Division.

17th BATTALION

ROYAL FUSILIERS

JULY 1917.

Army Form C. 2118.

WAR DIARY
14th ROYAL IRISH FUSILIERS
INTELLIGENCE SUMMARY.
(Erase heading not required.)

July 21

Place	Date	Hour	Summary of Events and Information	Remarks and references to Appendices
CANAL LEFT. (PONT FIXE)	1-2		Hostile wiring party dispersed by Lewis gun fire. Patrols of pumping head near Tunny crater; on subsequent enquiry from the tunnelling office it would appear that this was coming from a known mine-shaft which was effectively countered by a mine of our own. The morale of the left company is now restored & that S.O.S. message was sent up by means of a pistol-ram rocket, provoking an immediate outburst of German hate.	
	3	12.30 a.m. to 1.30 a.m.	DEATH OR GLORY RAID (C.Coy.) was received by a party of about 30 men after a few mortar barrage. They approached in two parties, one along the canal bank and one on the northern boundary of the sap. Both parties were repulsed by machine gun and Lewis gun fire leaving two dead. They managed to evacuate their wounded. C.oy received the congratulations of the Brigade, Divisional and Corps commanders. The following decorations were awarded - Lieut. H.H.AYSCOUGH Military Cross and 4190 P/c W.WHITSON Military Medal. Nightly patrols to discover enemy posts. None are sheds, and fishing am the Basse Canal until No. 5 Mills springers officially forbidden. A new signal office erected at Battalion headquarters and a house put into a state of defence for	
	4-10			

Army Form C. 2118.

WAR DIARY
1st Royal Fusiliers
INTELLIGENCE SUMMARY.
(Erase heading not required.)

July

Place	Date	Hour	Summary of Events and Information	Remarks and references to Appendices
CANAL LEFT (PONTFIXE)			The greater experience of the same headquarters during hostile artillery activity.	
	11-15		Several enemy M.G. and T.M. emplacements spotted. Several enemy working parties seen opposite various points of our front. They gave our Lewis guns and snipers plenty of practice and hits are claimed.	
LE PREOL	16	9p.m	Battalion was relieved by the 24th R. Fusiliers and went back to LE PREOL where all ranks found comfortable billets awaiting them.	
	17-21		Very little time was available for training as parties had to be supplied for BRADDEL CASTLE, MOUNTAIN KEEP and SPOIL BANK. Working Parties and Carrying Parties had also to be found every night – with the result that two Companies were always in the line. When Companies were not engaged in this work they were able to carry out some firing practices on the full range at LE QUESNOY which was at the disposal of the Battalion for eight hours everyday on this day.	
CANAL LEFT 2			Battalion returned to the trenches taking over from the 24th R. Fusiliers	

WAR DIARY
17th ROYAL FUSILIERS
INTELLIGENCE SUMMARY

Army Form C. 2118.

Place	Date	Hour	Summary of Events and Information	Remarks and references to Appendices
CANAL LEFT (PONT FIXE)	23 July		No event of importance took place.	
	24		Enemy raided on the extreme left of our front with revolvers surprised the three men who garrisoned the LEFT POST in EAST SORREY CRATER. Despite the fact that our men were taken completely unawares they put up a desperate struggle, one escaped back to give warning to those in the FRONT LINE. The other two were wounded and dragged back towards the REAR MAN LINE by their captors. Before reaching it, however, one of them broke away, and despite being wounded in two or our places, and in face of heavy Lewis gun fire from our own side, succeeded in regaining our lines. The Boche party was estimated at 9 men, 1 of whom was left dead in our SAP Head. Identification proved him to belong to the 1st Bavarian Reserve Infantry Regt; which was in accordance with the normal disposition in this part of the line. 51343 Pte H. JORDAN, the man who succeeded in escaping was awarded the MILITARY MEDAL.	SR SW
	25.26		Enemy wiring parties dispersed by our Lewis Gun fire. Enemy T.M.s active during stands by Battalions on our left and right.	SW

WAR DIARY

17th ROYAL or FUSILIERS
INTELLIGENCE SUMMARY.

(Erase heading not required.)

Army Form C. 2118.

Place	Date	Hour	Summary of Events and Information	Remarks and references to Appendices
CANAL LEFT (PONT FIXE)	July 27		Battalion boundary extended to the right "D" Coy. taking over a front, extending from S. BANK of the LA BASSÉE CANAL to Nos 14, 9 and 10. BRICKSTACKS inclusive, from the 2nd H.L.I.	sup.
	28/31		No event of particular importance occurred. Officers patrols sent out every night from each Company. Slight artillery activity on both sides.	ones.

C.F. Kerton S/Ldr
Commanding 17th R. Fusiliers

5th Brigade.

2nd Division.

17th BATTALION

ROYAL FUSILIERS

AUGUST 1917.

WAR DIARY or INTELLIGENCE SUMMARY.

Army Form C. 2118．

1/4th Royal Fusiliers

Place	Date	Hour	Summary of Events and Information	Remarks and references to Appendices
CANAL SECTION	2		The battalion was relieved by the 24th Royal Fusiliers and marched to LE PRÉOL. Box respirators were worn throughout the relief as a test.	S.A.
E PRÉOL	3-8		While in rest at LE PRÉOL the usual light training – bayonet fighting, physical training etc. – was carried out for two hours each day. Each company fired on the range at LE QUESNOY, and derived valuable rifles. A few cricket matches were played but the men were generally too exhausted after the long spell in the trenches to take part in organised sport.	
CANAL SECTION			Relieved the 24th in the CANAL SECTION	S.A.
	10/11		On the night of the 10/11 an enemy mining company exploded a mine near SURREY CRATER. The enemy occupied the crater.	S.A.
	11/11		On the night of the 11/12. 45 O.Rs rank and under 1/4 R.F, M.G. were detailed to retake the crater. 2 coys of the 2nd Royal Fusiliers and 2 coys of the 26th Royal Fusiliers, and later the line during the	S.A.

226

WAR DIARY or INTELLIGENCE SUMMARY

Army Form C. 2118.

Place: Arqueul
14th Royal Fusiliers

Place	Date	Hour	Summary of Events and Information	Remarks and references to Appendices

Operation. The party was divided into two waves. The first consisted of three parties of 15 O.R.'s each under an Officer. Stenhilhouse, Barker, and Schofield commanded the party. The second wave consisted of 30 other ranks in also supplied Mess'rs Lucas and Sherwood commanded this party. 6 rifle grenadiers cooperated in rear to resist any serious opposition. A special wire was laid to the front line and communication was not interrupted.

The attack started. The enemy vacated the crater, leaving two dead in our hands. All objectives were reached and three posts were established, when enemy parties worked the flanks of the posts and were not interrupted. A fresh counter-clay the posts were started. At 2.45 am the attacking troops were withdrawn and three post I Officer, 1 NCO and 6 men each remained with Lewis gunners. Our casualties amounted to 3 killed and 10 wounded. At 3.10 am

WAR DIARY
or
INTELLIGENCE SUMMARY.
(Erase heading not required.)

Army Form C. 2118.

1/4th Royal Fusiliers

Place	Date	Hour	Summary of Events and Information	Remarks and references to Appendices
Authuil			The enemy opened a heavy bombardment, lasting till 3.30 a.m. All ranks displayed a fine military spirit, and special praise is due to Major Hole, M.C. for his courage and organising ability. The undermentioned have been awarded the military medal in connection with the operations:— L/Sgt J Carrington, L/C O Lowry, Pte W Parker, Pte W Smith, Sergt A Bray, Cpl P Byres, L/C A Walley, L/C O Lowry, Pte W Parker. The battalion relieved the two coys of 1/? 24th R.F. who had held the line during the above operations south of	S.R. S.R. S.R. S.R.
	12		Took over the company frontage immediately south of the canal from the 9/H.L.I.	
LE PREOLU	13		Relieved by 2nd Royal Fusiliers and marched to LE PREOLU	

Army Form C. 2118.

WAR DIARY
or
INTELLIGENCE SUMMARY.
(Erase heading not required.)

Army Form: 17th Royal Fusiliers

Instructions regarding War Diaries and Intelligence Summaries are contained in F.S. Regs., Part II. and the Staff Manual respectively. Title pages will be prepared in manuscript.

Place	Date	Hour	Summary of Events and Information	Remarks and references to Appendices
LE PREOL	15		Pte H. Jordan and Lt. Clarke were awarded the Military Medal. The commanding officer addressed the regiment expressing his appreciation of its recent conduct in the line.	
		16.30	Tramps carried out. Two hours daily. Each Coy fired on the range. A lecture on the Spearman Army was delivered to all available officers. A voluntary service was held on the 19th.	
CANAL Section	20		Relieved the 24th R.F. in the Canal section, holding the line. No incident occurred during this tour in the line with the exception of intermittent shelling of the new ("WARLINGHAM") crater.	
KINGSCLERE	26		The battalion moved into Brigade Support, Hedges of KINGSCLERE (south of the canal), and coys at BRADBURY CASTLE, MOUNTAIN IN REEF, TOWER RESERVE, MARYLEBONE ROAD, ESPERANTO TERRACE, CAMBRIDGE TERRACE, SPOIL BANK and ORCHARD KEEP	

Army Form C. 2118.

WAR DIARY
or
INTELLIGENCE SUMMARY.
(Erase heading not required.)

Army: 14th Royal Fusiliers

Month: August

Place	Date	Hour	Summary of Events and Information	Remarks and references to Appendices
CANAL SECTOR 29	29		On the 29th, the battalion relieved the 24th R.F. in the canal section. The Portuguese troops attached to the battalion, were split up amongst the posts. During the night the following were killed:— 2/Lieut Drummond, Pte L. Jenner, Cpl E. Perkins, " D. Paisley, L/C D. Gordon, " A. Uttridge, Pte J. Dunn, " J. Finch. Pte R. Hart, " W. Wolfe, " G. Wilton, " F. Saunders, " E. Spear, " H. Brown. 24 other ranks were wounded. Ration Strength 31/8/14; 44 all ranks. Trench Strength 31/8/17; 36 + all ranks	

A.8834 Wt.W4973/M687 750,000 8/16 D. D. & L. Ltd. Forms/C.2118/13.

5th Brigade
2nd Division.

17th BATTALION

ROYAL FUSILIERS

SEPTEMBER 1917.

Army Form C. 2118.

WAR DIARY
or
INTELLIGENCE SUMMARY.
(Erase heading not required.)

17th Royal Fusiliers

September

Place	Date	Hour	Summary of Events and Information	Remarks and references to Appendices
CANAL LEFT	1/9/17 to 4/9		The Battalion completes a fifteen-day tour without further incident. Disposition handed over to 22nd Royal Fusiliers, normal: in addition Posts 28-29-30 on South Bank of Canal. The attached Coys of the 2/6 Battalion C.E.F. were sent back to BEUVRY without casualties.	
L PREOL	5/9		Usual day of rest. Coys at disposal of Coy Commanders for in town economy etc.	
	6/9		Range allotted to snipers and rifle section. Theatricals, "L BUFFNOT", hired by Battalion for concert. T/Major S.J.M. HOLE M.C. awarded bar to M.C. and C.Q.M.S.J.MEAD awarded M.M. for devotion to duty in connection with attack on WARLINGHENT CRATER 11/8/17.	
	7/9		Short route march by all Coys. Football match at 5.30 pm Regiment 3 "v" T.M. Battery	

WAR DIARY
INTELLIGENCE SUMMARY.

(Erase heading not required.)

Army Form C. 2118.

Instructions regarding War Diaries and Intelligence Summaries are contained in F.S. Regs., Part II. and the Staff Manual respectively. Title pages will be prepared in manuscript.

Place	Date	Hour	Summary of Events and Information	Remarks and references to Appendices
Le Preol	8/9		The Battalion shot on Inter Platoon and Revolver Competition at L.G.V.F. SNOY range. This competition is continued in D'mesnil.	
Canal Left.	9/9		Relieved the 24th Royal Fusiliers. Dispositions: "B" Coy in the Centre. "A" Centre. "D" Right, "C" Reserve.	
	10/9		Special "D" Coy. R.E. projected 650 drums of gas from the "Railway Bridge". Weak retaliation. Capt: T/Major J. BRETT, 2nd Bat. & Bucks Lgt Inft, posted to 2nd Bat. Bucks Lt. Inft as second in command. T/Major J. HOLE assumes duties second in command. 17th MGC.	
	11/9		Inter Company relief. Dispositions: "C" Right, "D" Left, "B" Reserve, "A" centre. Raid by 139th Lgt. Bde. on our right.	
Bde Reserve	12/9		Relieved by 24th R. Fus. and marched into Brigade Reserve line.	

Army Form C. 2118.

WAR DIARY
— or —
INTELLIGENCE SUMMARY.
(Erase heading not required.)

Instructions regarding War Diaries and Intelligence Summaries are contained in F. S. Regs., Part II. and the Staff Manual respectively. Title pages will be prepared in manuscript.

Place	Date	Hour	Summary of Events and Information	Remarks and references to Appendices
	19/9		Dispositions. Hqrs. Kingsclere. "A" Coy. Esplanade and Ranbury Rows. "B". Maybiloux Mountain Wigh and Roachwell Castle. "C". Sport Rach, Orchard Road, "D". Shaws Rd.	ap
	Night 19/20/9		"D" Coy R.E. projected 350 drums on the TORTOISE and the German support line.	ap
	19/9.		Partial Inter-Battalion relief. "A" Coy. from STIRLING SAP (inclusive) to S. bank of the Bases Canal (exclusive). "D" Coy. from SHAWS CUT to TO PEAS 70.5(?) The other two Coys. did not move.	ap
CANAL LEFT.	22/23/9		Relieved 2/4th R. Fus.	ap
	24.		Officers and representatives of the 1st Battalion, C.E.P, with instructors, arrived to be shown round the lines.	ap
	25/26/9		Relieved by 1st Batt. C.E.P. less "A" Coy. holding the Crater system.	ap

A5834 Wt. W4973/M687 750,000 8/16 D. D. & L. Ltd. Forms/C.2118/13.

Army Form C. 2118.

WAR DIARY
—or—
INTELLIGENCE SUMMARY.
(Erase heading not required.)

Place	Date	Hour	Summary of Events and Information	Remarks and references to Appendices
BEUVRY.	28/9.		The Battalion marched to BEUVRY. "C" Coy relieved "A" Coy in the line.	
	29/9		A.B.D. Coys through Gas Chamber, 50 ORE.	
	29/9/19		"C" Coy 17th R.Fus relieved by "D" Coy 24th R.Fus.	
	29/9.		Coys march independently to Le PREOL and take up their usual billets.	
Le PREOL	30/9.		Voluntary service. — All Coys on the range. — The following officer reinforcements joined the Battalion :— 2/Lts. VICKERS, HEAD, ASHWELL, FELTON, WINN, HARDRESS, McGREGOR. Robert Fleight Lt Col Comd 17th R Fusiliers	

5th Brigade.

2nd Division

17th BATTALION

ROYAL FUSILIERS

OCTOBER 1917.

WAR DIARY

Army Form C. 2118.

17TH ROYAL FUSILIERS

OCTOBER

Place	Date	Hour	Summary of Events and Information	Remarks
LE PREOL	1.10.17		T/Capt. J. AYLMER returned to duty with the Battalion	
	2.10.17		T/Major S.J.M. HOLE. M.C. assumes command of the Battalion during the temporary absence of T/Lt.Col. S.V.P. WESTON. D.S.O. M.C. on 2nd of leave to England. Baths at the disposal of the Battalion.	
		8 p.m.	Open air entertainment by the Fans in orchard adjacent to H.Q. Mess; slight suspicions caused by raiding enemy aircraft.	
	3.10.17		Special platoon of "B" Coy. fired off final in Brigade Lewis Gun Competition. Battalion sports in afternoon.	
	4.10.17		All Coys. at disposal of Coy. Commanders.	
		6.15 p.m.	The Battalion moves up to relieve the 24th R. Fus. in the CANAL LEFT SUBSECTOR. Dispositions 'A' Coy. Left, 'D' Centre, 'C' Right. 'B' Coy. VILLAGE LINE (PONT FIXE). Extra officers returned to rear H.Q. Mess at LE QUESNOY.	
CANAL LEFT	5.10.17		'D' Coy (Special) R.E. projects 450 Drums of Gas.	
	6.10.17		Battalion relieved by the 2nd Bn SOUTH LANCS. Regt. & marched back to Billets in BETHUNE	

Army Form C. 2118.

WAR DIARY
or
INTELLIGENCE SUMMARY.
(Erase heading not required.)

17th ROYAL FUSILIERS

OCTOBER

Place	Date	Hour	Summary of Events and Information	Remarks and references to Appendices
BETHUNE	7.10.17		Kit inspection by all Coys. Advance party under 2/Lt Wright proceeded to MARLES LES MINES	
	8.10.17		The Brigade marched via CHOCQUES to MARLES LES MINES area. The Battn went into billets at LAPUGNOY.	
LAPUGNOY	9.10.17		Coys at disposal of Coy commanders for re-organisation in four platoon basis. Inoculation by Coys throughout the day.	
	10.10.17		Coys at disposal of Coy commanders. Arrival of a staff of 34 O.R's. Training according to programme. Lecture for officers at 5.30 pm.	
	11.10.17		" " Each Coy a Rifle Range for 2 hours.	
	12.10.17		All Coys - "The Company in Attack" Specialyst classes as usual. Lecture 5.30	
	13.10.17		Voluntary services in the Divisional Theatre (Village Hall). Battn at CHOCQUES at disposal of the Battalion.	
	14.10.17		Lt Col. S.V.P. WESTON DSO. MC. relinquished command of the Battalion on return from short leave to England. The Brigade was inspected by the Army Commander at MARLES LES MINES - The Battalion being on the right of the Brigade.	
	15.10.17			

WAR DIARY
INTELLIGENCE SUMMARY.

17TH ROYAL FUSILIERS

OCTOBER

Army Form C. 2118.

Place	Date	Hour	Summary of Events and Information	Remarks and references to Appendices
LAPUGNOY	16.10.17		Usual Training programme. Lecture by Bde. Gas Officer to all Officers & NCOs at 5.30p	
	17.10.17		" " " including interior sigging. Staff was watched including some American Staff Officers.	
			1st & 2nd Sun appreciation by some American Staff Officers.	
			Results of Brigade Lewis Gun & Platoon Competition published. The Battalion won 1st & 2nd Lewis Gun & Platoon Competition with scores of 79 & 1090 respectively.	
			The Divisional Competition was fired off at AUCHEL – The Battalion finished second in both parts – only 4½ points out of 1680 behind the winners the 1st K.R.R.	
	19.10.17		Usual Training programme.	CofS
	19.10.17		" " " Lecture to Officers & NCO's by Brig Gen. Bullen Smith CMG, DSO Staff	
	20.10.17		Battn R.o.E. Lewis to Rifle Range	CofS
	21.10.17		Usual Voluntary Services.	CofS
	22.10.17		Brigade in attack across ALLOUAGNE – LAPUGNOY Road.	
			2/Lt. A. FORBES MENZIES rejoins the Battn. & was posted to "C" Coy	CofS
			2/Lt. F. KITELEY reports for duty & was appointed Signalling Officer.	
	23.10.17		Usual Training programme – One Coy on Rifle Range	CofS
	24.10.17		" " " including firing	

Army Form C. 2118.

WAR DIARY
or
INTELLIGENCE SUMMARY
(Erase heading not required.)

OCTOBER   17TH ROYAL FUSILIERS

Place	Date	Hour	Summary of Events and Information	Remarks and references to Appendices
LA PUGNOY	25/10/17	4 a.m.	Coys. paraded for Battalion Training in Attack at Dawn	Extn
			Later all Coys. tested fox respirators in gas hut.	
	26.10.17		Company & Platoon Training. 'A' Coy. on Rifle Range	SiR
			Lecture by M.O. on "First Aid" at 5.30 p.m.	
	27.10.17		Battalion parade	SiR
	28.10.17		"Voluntary" Services as usual	SiR
	29.10.17		Usual training programme	SiR
	30.10.17		" " Coys in attack.	SiR
	31.10.17		The Battalion marched to the Rifle Range & practised the attack.	SiR
			Ration Strength Officers 39	
			O.R. 729	

Endorsed
for D
5/11/17
Cmdg 17 R. Fusiliers

5th Brigade.
2nd Division.

17th BATTALION

ROYAL FUSILIERS

NOVEMBER 1917.

Army Form C. 2118.

WAR DIARY
or
INTELLIGENCE SUMMARY
(Erase heading not required.)

17th ROYAL FUSILIERS

Place	Date	Hour	Summary of Events and Information	Remarks and references to Appendices
LAPUGNOY	1/11/17		Training. Special instruction to :- Snipers (16 per Battalion), Trench Mortars, Lewis Gunners. The ranges are very much used and good results obtained. The new drafts have settled down. They are of good physique and seem well trained. Prepare to move to YPRES.	
	5/11/17		Marched to Thiennes. Nobody fell out. (20 Kilometres.)	
THIENNES	6/11/17		Continued on. Favoured by good weather but mile of pavé stones which temporarily knocked up some of the men fit. The Division moves into the II Corps - (15 Kilometres)	
ST SYLVESTRE CAPPEL	7/11/17			
ZERNEZEELE	8/11/17		Marched through CASSEL to Zernezeele area. Companies much scattered but good billets. (10 Kilometres)	
			Only small Company training grounds. Prepare to stay here for a short time. Training under Coy Commanders. Short route marches after dark in gas helmets. Successful sports meeting under Battalion arrangements. Prepare to move —	
	14/11/17		Marched to Winnizeele (12 Kilometres). Very bad mud. Camp in plowed field. 'A' and 'B' Coys some distance away. Clearing camp of mud except nearest two	
WINNIZEELE	15/11/17			
	16/11/17		days. Lectures by O.C. Bd N.o.W. etc. to officers nightly. Football match. 2nd to Y.A.F.A. by 1 goal.	

WAR DIARY
or
INTELLIGENCE SUMMARY.

17th ROYAL FUSILIERS.

Army Form C. 2118

Place	Date	Hour	Summary of Events and Information	Remarks and references to Appendices
WINNEZEELE	21/11/17		Route march in full pack.	
	28/11/17		Demonstration of mud grenade rockets. Not very successful. Coys in attack under their Commanders - Commanders made out our elaborate schemes. Rumours that the Division will go to ITALY.	
Night	26/13/11/17		Marched to CASSEL Station and entrained for ACHIET-LE-GRAND.	
BEAULENCOURT			Man into IV Corps - marched to BEAULENCOURT. Division went up to consolidate line in General Byng's advance.	
FABEUQUIERES	25/11/17		A Nissen camp here.	
HERMIES	26/11/17		Moved to old British line - Relieved 15th R.I.R.	
BURTON WOOD	27/11/17		Relieved 22nd R.Fus. same day in KANGAROO Trench E.28 Central. and attached to 99th Inf. Bde.	
	28/11/17		Relieved 1st K.R.R. in the front line, Battalion HQ at E.22.d.1.0.0.	
	29/11/17		1st K.R.R. attacked through us at dawn and straightened out the line through E.2.2.1.b. D. Coy. took over this new piece of line at about	

Army Form C. 2118.

WAR DIARY
or
INTELLIGENCE SUMMARY.
(Erase heading not required.)

17th ROYAL FUSILIERS —

Place	Date	Hour	Summary of Events and Information	Remarks and references to Appendices
	30/11/17		Relieved by 2th R. Fus. at 10 p.m. and rejoined the 5th Inf. Bde. in K14.	
			Casualties —	
			10 Officers and 167 O.Rs.	
			Killed.	
			Capt William Stone.	
			Lt Solomon BENZECRY.	
			2Lt CYRIL YELLEN	
			2Lt Arthur SHERWOOD.	
			Missing.	
			2Lt Arthur COCKER.	
			Wounded.	
			2Lt John LUCAS.	Soho
			2Lt EDWARD CHITTENDEN	
			2Lt WILLIAM H. HAFFIE.	
			2Lt FRANK RITELEY.	
			1Lt ALBERT McGREGOR.	Sho
			1Lt ERNEST BARDER.	
			Ration Strength — 22 Officers A61 O.R.	
			Trench " 20 Officers 351 O.R.	
			Cas Lists JWL	
			Lt Col R. ??????	
			Cmd 17th R Fus 3/12/17

Army Form C. 2118.

WAR DIARY
or
INTELLIGENCE SUMMARY.
(Erase heading not required.)

17th ROYAL FUSILIERS

Place	Date	Hour	Summary of Events and Information	Remarks and references to Appendices
Front Line	30/11/17		Enemy mass attack at 9 A.M. Fierce hand to hand fighting for five hours. The Battalion gave no ground. Line of resistance changed during the battle. The Battalion bore the brunt of the fighting and undoubtedly saved the whole line from breaking. No reinforcements reached us. Rough sketch showing Battalion dispositions (A) at commencement, (B) at finish of battle.	

"A"
GERMAN FRONT LINE.
"B" "C" "D"
Line showing direction of retirement by three alternate Coys. over the open.
1st K.R.R. East Hy. 1st R. Berks R.

"B"
GERMAN FRONT LINE.
Direction of main thrust by enemy.
OBLOCKS
C. GARDEN
1st K.R.R. at "A" "B" "D" 1st R. Berks R.
GARDENS

Copy   1.12.17.

My dear Weston,

Words can in no way express my thanks to and admiration of you and your magnificent battalion for your splendid behaviour throughout the enemy attack of yesterday.

You bore the brunt of the attack, and the divisional commander tells me that ten successive waves of Germans attempted to break through our line.

Please convey my very deep thanks to my old comrades of the 17th with whom I served for 7 months in England.

You have covered yourself with glory in every action you have taken part in.

As for yourself - your leading, and conduct of affairs could not be surpassed, and your information (most of which unfortunately miscarried and only reached me at midnight last night) was more than helpful.

                                        Yours ever,
                                        R.O. Kellett.

17/Royal Fusiliers - Cambrai 1917.

(Extracts from Note Book of Br.-Gen. S.V.P. Weston).

99th push forward posts in front of trench between E.17.d.35 and E.23.a.31.

On night 30th Nov/1st Dec. 99th will establish 3 posts between E.22.a.55 and the N.E. corner of round trench at inter-brigade boundary E.21.b.72 and two supporting posts in rear of these.

On the same night 6th Inf. Bde. will carry out similar operation on their side.

All posts to be dug in by night: occupied by day and night. Strength of all posts to be 1 Lewis gun detachment and 10 rifles.

Patrol 22a. and reconnoitre to 21.b.72.

Relieved by 5th on 4/5th.

Establish post at E.22.b.4.4.

O.C. "D" Coy.

You will relieve "C" Coy K.R.R. in the line to-night under Coy. arrangements.
The line to be taken over will run from the aeroplane at E.23.a.1.1. approx. to E.22.central.
If possible an advance post will be made at E.22.b.6.1. A patrol will first be sent forward to ascertain the feasibility of this.
The line will be consolidated with a series of strong posts and wired in front. Gaps will be left in the wire for patrols. $\frac{1}{2}$ coy of the D.C.L.I. will be at your disposal for wiring and consolidation.
Tools will be handed over by the 1st K.R.R.
$\frac{1}{2}$ coy "C" Coy D.C.L.I. will report to you about 10.30 p.m.
The relief will commence as soon as it is sufficiently dark.

O.C. "B" Coy.

It is of vital importance to the Bde. to ascertain if the ground round E.22.a.0.0. is or is not clear of the enemy.
You will send out an officer's patrol to-night to ascertain:
    (1) the nature of the ground.
    (2) the presence or absence of enemy.
    (3) whether or not there is any wire which would prove an obstacle in any direction.

29.11.17.
3.5 p.m.   S.V.P.Weston, Lt.-Col.

O.C. "D".

You will hold on to your present line at all costs.

The main line of resistance will be from 22.b.82 to 22.b.02.
The attack is a pretty big one.
I am withdrawing most of A. & B. & C from the Rats Tail to consolidate the main line of resistance in rear of you. In the main line C will be on the right, in touch with the Berks. A. will be in the centre. B. will be on the left in touch with K.R.R. Consolidation will be in depth on the main line of resistance.

30.11.17.
10.25 a.m.
         S.V.P. Weston, Lt.-Col.

99th Inf. Bde.

 My line now established as per attached map.
 Have obtained touch with K.R.R. on left.
 Have no information about touch on the right.
 Can obtain no further news about enemy bringing up artillery as the officer (sentence unfinished)
 The Bosch are now on the crest of the hill at E.22.b.5.2.
 I doubt if my line will hold.
 Have blocked trench at E.22.C.9.5. and am holding up Bosch there.
 My main line has gone from about E.22.D.5.8.
 Am preparing a defensive flank down this trench from E.22.C.92 to road.

99th Inf. Bde.

 My line is still holding.
 Judging by the line of the enemy's advance I should say that my left flank, i.e. K.R.R. had gone.
 Have made defensive flank to road but want reinforcements and above all ammunition.
 Am neither in touch on right flank or left flank but my line is holding.
 Ammunition urgent.

30th.
11.50 a.m.
         S.V.P. Weston, Lt.-Col.
          17th R.F.

99th Inf. Bde.

 My line is still holding.
 K.R.R. line on my left is still holding.
 No news of the Berks on my right.
 Am urgently in need of bombs to hold the block and ammunition.
 The German guns are lengthening their range.
 My men are in fine fettle but it is a question of whether you can get me bombs and ammunition and reinforcements before the next enemy attack.
 I have only about 6 officers left and my casualties are very heavy.
 One of our heavies is still firing short by B.H.Q.

30th.
12.10 p.m.
         S.V.P. Weston, Lt.-Col.
          17th R.F.

99th Inf. Bde.   4th Message.

    Am in touch with K.R.R. on my left.
    Am in touch with 23rd R.F. on my right.
    My main line of resistance is holding firm, but I have not sufficient men left to consolidate in depth.
    The enemy now holds the line captured by K.R.R. yesterday (approx.).
    The enemy appears to be consolidating on this line, also in front of the K.R.R. on my left.
    Apparently the attack did not reach the K.R.R. on my left.
    See attached map for general situation.
    No reinforcements, bombs, or ammunition have yet arrived.

30th.   S.V.P. Weston, Lt.-Col.
1 p.m.   17th R.F.

99th Inf. Bde.

    My officers are quite confident that they can hold the line with more ammunition.
    The men, of course, are very exhausted as they fought with the Germans with the bayonet but full of fight still. One company fought with the bayonet till only 20 men were left.
    My line is now rather mixed with K.R.R. and 23rd R.F.
    Our guns are shooting short at E.22.b.9.0. which is my right flank and where I still have a post.
    Can you send me a 3-inch Stokes Mortar gun as I have found a dump of ammunition. It would help to defend my double block.

99th Inf. Bde.   6th Message.

    The situation remains unchanged.
    The enemy aeroplanes are once more up in large numbers.
    I have only 5 Lewis guns left in action.
    I have no brigade machine guns as far as I can ascertain still left in action.
    I have heard no word from the brigade since the action commenced.
    A reliable sergt. reports to me that the Bosch look as if they were about to attack again on my left where the K.R.R. are holding the line.

30th Nov.   S.V.P. Weston, Lt.-Col.
2.50 p.m.   17th R.F.

    I had already asked K.R.R. about half an hour ago to consolidate their line in depth. Their men have not yet arrived but should do so any minute.

99th Inf. Bde.   7th Message.

    Coy. Commander on my right flank reports that the enemy are preparing for another attack.
    He is shooting at him as he is forming up.
    We shall hold on at all costs.
    This information comes from a reliable source.

30th Nov.   S.V.P. Weston, Lt.-Col.
           Cmdg. 17th R.Fusiliers.
3.40 p.m.   This message sent also by pigeon.

8th Message.

There is no carbon copy of this message, but at the foot of the page "This message was sent also by pigeon".

99th Inf. Bde.   9th Message.

Enemy is counter-attacking heavily down trench leading to 22 Central. If you can get a battery on the trench from 22.a.9.4. to 22.C.8.8. we shall wipe them out.
    The trench is full of Bosch.
    My blocks are still holding.
    My right coy. reports that they had a man in from the 47th Div. They suspect him of being a spy as he has disappeared.

30th.   S.V.P. WESTON,
4.25 p.m.   Lt.-Col.

    Have just got on direct to artillery and arranged for them to plaster the trench in question.
                                              S.V.P.W.

99th Bde.

    The situation is once more normal.
    I think that the Bosch is relieving now.
    My relief has not yet arrived but is expected at every moment.

30th.   S.V.P. Weston, Lt.-Col.
5 p.m.   17th R. Fusiliers.

Addenda to evidence of Capt. Stones' recommendation:

    It has been a matter of great difficulty to secure the best evidence of this gallant officer's actions. Of the rearguard who remained with him there is no survivor.
    Up to the time when the line was cut Capt. Stone continued to send the clearest and most concise, and as it was afterwards proved, most accurate messages to myself at B.H.Q.

Dec. 1917.   S.V.P. Weston, Lt.-Col.
                         Comdg. 17th R. Fusiliers.

    Stong points will be well wired. 40 yds out esp. on flanks. Capable of all round resistance. Dumps will be formed of S.A.A., bombs, Very lights, tools and wire and water.
    Protracted resistance.
    Machine-gun support.

4.30.   Report rec'd from O.C. "D".
           Thick mist.

4.32.   Artillery could not be informed.

4.33.   Bde. informed.

4.35.   24th informed.

6 p.m.   F. Leggett arrives.

6.30 p.m. Stokes mortars arrived. Ordered to put a
           gun to enfilade Trench at 3.C.9.0. Artillery
           ordered to get on to Slag heap.

6.30.   Bde. informed that we have lost our code calls.
           Bde. defer action for the night, order
           Ox & Bucks to relieve with us.

7.10.   Ox & B. not arrived.

7.45.   Stokes Mortar bombs not detonated.
           Ox & Bucks arrive.

5th Inf. Bde.

    Reference Defence Scheme.

    My Right Front Coy. is 10 O.R, short and my Left Front Coy. is 12 O.R. short of the numbers laid down by whom the posts were to be held. There is no Reserve in either Coy available for immediate counter-attack.
    The same will apply when the two coys now in support come into the line.
    We shall withdraw all our working parties at 3 p.m. tomorrow. Are a corresponding number please to be withdrawn from the 24th R.F. to relieve them at this hour ?
    For your information please.

19.12.17.   S.V.P. Weston, Lt.-Col.

    The two front coys will each send out a patrol every night under mutual arrangements so as not to clash. All posts and flank Batt. posts will be warned.
    Every post will have a single sentry by day, and a double sentry by night. The men will work in the vicinity of their post.
    The coy in close support will have 1 platoon ready for immediate counter-attack.
    Touch will be established and maintained on the flanks.
    There will be no movement over the top by day. Rifle bolts will be constantly worked at night to avoid freezing.
    Two beds will be available at the Aid Post for officers in the front line, one for each coy.

5th Inf. Bde.

    Reference Albert Gate.

    On visiting this post last night I found a small shell hole which combined every defect that it would be possible to concentrate into so small a space.
(1) The shell hole is 1' 6" deep with a diameter about 6 feet.
(2) It is exactly 32 paces in a N.E. direction from JILL.

    In its present position I would suggest please that it can serve no purpose whatever except in view of your GS 740/489 to lead perhaps to ridicule.

Owing to its shallow depth the men occupying it can be seen long before they can see anyone.

The wire in front of JILL would impede their retirement unless they struck the gap immediately.

The enemy would be on them so quickly as to make it impossible to telephone and difficult to retire.

I ordered the shell hole to be deepened to furnish protection while I sent out a patrol to find the trenches about K.2.c.5.2. Owing to the thick mist the patrol was not successful.

I would suggest please
(1) The post be abolished altogether and the telephone kept in JILL.
(2) The post be established in trenches about K.2.c.5.2 if found by patrols to be unoccupied by the enemy.

Can I have some instructions please.

21.12.17.
                S.V.P. Weston, Lt.-Col.
                Comdg. 17th R. Fusiliers.

Fighting Patrol.

One officer, 1 Sgt. 1 Cpl, and 10 O.R's to start at 5 a.m. from Joan: work due north to 2 central: catch Bosch working party. Then turn due E. to trench in 2.A.50 and work home south and reconnoitre along trench. Men to carry two bombs, rifle and bayonet and ammunition in pocket.

All identification to be left behind.
All flank coys and batts. warned.
Organisation. Particular attention paid to flanks and rear.
Object. To get identification.
Men to rest at B.H.Q. Hot food provided.
Officer to take compass and keep in centre of patrol.
No bombs to be thrown unless unavoidable.
Photos and maps to be studied.
Two stretcher bearers to remain in Joan.
Two men to carry a ground sheet.

NOTE: Remainder of note book contains hints to officers and N.C.O's on their rôles, presumably notes of lectures to them at various times.

5th Brigade.
2nd Division.

17th BATTALION

ROYAL FUSILIERS

DECEMBER 1917.

Army Form C. 2118.

WAR DIARY
or
INTELLIGENCE SUMMARY. 17th ROYAL FUSILIERS
(Erase heading not required.)

Instructions regarding War Diaries and Intelligence Summaries are contained in F. S. Regs., Part II. and the Staff Manual respectively. Title pages will be prepared in manuscript.

Place	Date	Hour	Summary of Events and Information	Remarks and references to Appendices
Old Battalion front line.	1/12		Rested here for ten days - No ammunition - Refitting and drew new Lewis guns. Remainder of Battalion in advent near BOURLON wood etc.	S/R
Lock 6.	3rd		Relieved 2/5 WEST RIDINGS in drug-outs round Lock Six - Plenty of room and rest for the men.	S/R
	4th		Retired to a line in front of Lock Seven which in a few days will be our front and main line of resistance. The retirement has already begun. Guns in front of un Jerry have destruction of dug-outs etc - Our Battalion working all night pushing to consolidate the line. 71st Div West of CANAL	S/R 37 -?
	5th		On the 4th/5th in our Left. The enemy has discovered that we are retiring and at 11.30 AM put down a heavy barrage on BOURSIES, N.E of 9th divisional front, and attacked in conjunction with another push further south. The line we occupy at the HINDENBURG support line - Plenty of dug-outs. The line we and at 10 am our own	S/R
	6th		Enemy advancing in small further all along the line front the troops - Rear guards withdraw through us as we became front line troops -	S/R

A.5834 Wt. W4973/M687 750,000 8/16 D. D. & L. Ltd. Forms/C.2118/13.

WAR DIARY
INTELLIGENCE SUMMARY. 17th ROYAL FUSILIERS.

Army Form C. 2118

Place	Date	Hour	Summary of Events and Information	Remarks and references to Appendices
FRONT LINE	7th		At 1 A.M. we are ordered to establish three posts roughly 500' in front of the line to be held at all costs. 3 pts. nothing are reported to be dug in them. Unable to find them by night but did them by dawn and near them. The R.E. did not arrive. Lt WATERS wounded on a carrying party. C.O., M.O., M=D.L. wounded by a shell near the transport lines at VELU WOOD, died of wounds. He was one of the most popular N.C.O.s in the battalion and was the M.M. at BEAUMONT HAMEL. Enemy reported to be in dark Side at 7pm. Enemy small parties.	S.P.s
	8th		In touch with enemy at 9 AM. 2/Lts WHITSON and LOWRY make gallant attempt to capture some Germans but unable to run fast enough. Intermittent bombing fight all day but no serious attack. Enemy more active on West of Canal. Enemy reinforced front line and shelled our frontage heavily all night.	S.P.s
	9th		Fighting again in the morning and though out the day. Enemy reported massing in front of us. He brings up medium trench mortar and causes us a good share of annoyance. Guns have not yet arrived. Relieved by 17th Battn MIDDLESEX REGIMENT and marched to LA BOUEGUIERE. A NISSEN camp. Men very tired and exhausted.	O.R.s

Frontage handed over 800'

Army Form C. 2118.

WAR DIARY
or
INTELLIGENCE SUMMARY. 17th ROYAL FUSILIERS.
(Erase heading not required.)

Place	Date	Hour	Summary of Events and Information	Remarks and references to Appendices
	9th		This completes a tour of fourteen days in the line; during which time the Battalion has fought the biggest battle in its history, undertaken constant relief and continuous minor enterprises against the enemy's front troops. On all occasions it has done magnificently and returns to a well earned rest and the highest praises from the Divisional and Brigade (with 99th and 5th) Commanders.	S/R
LABUQUIÈRE	10th		Interview ced. Baths and clean underclothing. Kit inspections.	S/R
	11th		Companies reorganized on the two platoon system. Lewis Gun training. Small working party for dug-outs.	S/R
HERMIES	14th To 19th		Battalion working on infantry line near HERMIES and at dusk moved into the village into Reserve. Relieved 17th Middlesex Regt & found accommodation.	S/R
			Small working parties. Large amount of work on Tunny the white-	S/R
Front line	20th		Relieved 2nd R. Fus. for a nine day tour in the left battalion sector of	S/R

WAR DIARY

17th ROYAL FUSILIERS

Place	Date	Hour	Summary of Events and Information	Remarks and references to Appendices
West of ENNAL in BARRAI sector.	21st		the Left Brigade. Snow on the ground – Battalion frontage about 2000x. We have four posts in front of main line of resistance average distance away 300x. The enemy has not yet found our exact position and is at least 800x away in places. All officers reconnoitring under cover of heavy fog – 3 reaches fairly good and clear, but not deep enough yet – Continuous belt of wire – Orders received from Brigade to send out a fighting patrol to secure identification – At 10 A.M. the enemy estimated at 30 rifles raided our front evening the west flank of battalion. Beaten off without loss and left one prisoner in our hands. A new kind of automatic pistol was found afterwards, probably belonging to the officer or N.C.O. i/c party, with a magazine containing 32 rounds. Unfortunately the pistol was damaged by our fire. It is interesting to note that the enemy failed to "push off" our front owing to the fact that they forgot to pull the strings of their bombs before throwing. Our men discovered	

Army Form C. 2118.

WAR DIARY
or
INTELLIGENCE SUMMARY. 1/7th ROYAL FUSILIERS
(Erase heading not required.)

Place	Date	Hour	Summary of Events and Information	Remarks and references to Appendices
Front line	12th		and fired on the enemy before they threw, nevertheless three bombs fell in the trench at the feet of our men – "D" Company continued the attack	S/R
			At 5 A.M. our fighting patrol went out to discover if the enemy was holding a trench some distance away but owing to the fog, which had been thick in the early morning for some days past, lifting, had to return earlier than expected and found no trace of the enemy – Rest of the day passed quietly –	S/R
	25th		A Xmas dinner held in H.Q. dug-out – 10 men per Company attended – The R.S.M. was wounded at 8.30 pm standing in the entrance to his dug-out with his servant and bugler. His toes is deeply felt and we trust he will not be absent more than a few months –	S/R
	26th		Relieved by the 1/8th Battalion ARGYLE and SUTHERLAND HIGHLANDERS and moved back to SANDERS Camp at O.A.B. During the very severe weather only six men were evacuated sick	S/R

WAR DIARY
or
INTELLIGENCE SUMMARY. 17th 19 ROYAL FUS 12/72

Army Form C. 2118.

(Erase heading not required.)

Place	Date	Hour	Summary of Events and Information	Remarks and references to Appendices
SANDERS Camp	27th		which is attributed to the fact that they were served with hot soup and cocoa at 8pm and 3am respectively -	
	28th		Camp not emptied and no conveniences - Baths and preparation for Xmas dinners -	
	29th		Officers Xmas dinner. "A" and "B" Company given Xmas dinner. Turkeys, geese and plum pudding, out of Canteen funds -	
	30th		"C" and "D" Coys. Xmas dinner. Review orders to attack under one hour's notice at 1pm. Our Bn was ordered near GOUZEAUCOURT - Cancelyd at 9pm. The arrangements made were successful. DR. Signallers, Runners and details dinner -	
	31st		Ration strength 24 Officers 489 O.R. Casualties - 1 Officers wounded 2 hurt F.G. WATERS 6 other ranks Killed 25 do wounded	

Signed
Lieut Col
Commanding 17th R.Fus B.

5th Brigade.
2nd Division.

Transferred to 5th Brigade 7.2.18.

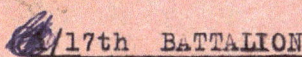/17th BATTALION

ROYAL FUSILIERS

JANUARY 1918.

WAR DIARY
or
INTELLIGENCE SUMMARY

Army Form C. 2118.

R F Vol 27 17th R?

Place	Date	Hour	Summary of Events and Information	Remarks and references to Appendices
Sanders Camp	Jan 1st		Severe frost still continues. Co. Training as far as conditions allowed. Musketry, Physical & bayonet fighting & active form of exercise.	App
	2nd		Same conditions. Same Training.	App
	3rd		The following were mentioned in the New Year Honours: See L? H.S. Havelock S/Lt A.? Menzies R.Q.M.S. T. Brunton C.S.M. H. Matthews S.S.I. C. Luke	App
			Batt. vacated billets & marched to BEADLENCOURT. During the stay at SANDERS CAMP the weather was exceptionally severe. A great difficulty was experienced in keeping the men warm. To do this an innovation for men starting out was introduced. Permission was given to collect wood for burning from French villages every day on arriving past new Sank at BARASTRE for the purpose. The scheme worked extremely well & added greatly to the comfort of troops.	App
BEADLENCOURT C CAMP	4th		Training commenced. Particular attention paid to musketry. All Subaltern Officers for Arthyl & Rifle Camp Musketry.	App
	5th		10 Offrs & 50 O.R's proceeded to BAPAUME for Rifles. Coen. Course Training continued. Too much snow & cold for same.	App

Place	Date	Hour	Summary of Events and Information	Remarks and references to Appendices
BEAULINCOURT Camp	Jan 6		Usual Sunday Service.	
			The following were awarded decorations for the fight of CAMBRAI on Nov 30th	
			Lt Col D.P. WESTON DSO MC BAR & DSO	
			Lt A.J. MENZIES DSO	
			Capt L.M. GLASSON MC	
			1st Lt W.J. LUCAS MC	
			2nd Lt W.T. HUGHES MC	
			2nd Lt C.F. DONCASTER MC	
			631 R.S.M. HAINES. A. BAR & DCM	
			608 S/S A. DRAY MM DCM	
			5662 Cpl WYNNE WT DCM	
			6218 S/S BENSON J K MM	
			1543 CSM S. LEcock G MM	
			1421 L/SGT DOHERTY B MM	
			1441 Pte PEARS. H J MM	
			5944 CSM STANLEY G MM	
			6846 Pte BISHOPP. S MM	
			353 L/C GUNSON T C MM	
			11962 Pte GIBSON. R MM	
			9067 L/Sgt GRINDROD W MM	
			1338 L/C GARDNER HS MM	
			48451 Sgt GRIMES T MM	
			11374 Pte MUTTITT WE MM	
			11611 Pte BRADFORD C BAR & MM	
			49359 Pte AARON CJ	

Army Form C. 2118.

WAR DIARY
or
INTELLIGENCE SUMMARY.
(Erase heading not required.)

Instructions regarding War Diaries and Intelligence Summaries are contained in F. S. Regs., Part II. and the Staff Manual respectively. Title pages will be prepared in manuscript.

Place	Date	Hour	Summary of Events and Information	Remarks and references to Appendices
BEAULINCOURT "C" CAMP	Jan 7th		Training continued but handicapped by severe cold. Worked 160 yard rifle range completed.	
	8th		Training Programme continued	
	9th		Leave started to AMIENS for 9 O.R. daily from 5.30 AM to 10 PM. Systematic collection of Waste Paper begun.	
	10th		Owing to severe snow bombing in the neighbourhood, all training suspended & unit concentrated on putting the huts. This was done by digging a trench midway between the huts & piling up the earth against the side of the hut, look on plan giving about to the hard ground. The plan has to be dept. 9 in. below the post.	
	11th		Palestine Yr[?]. continued Camp rechained JERICHO CAMP.	
JERICHO CAMP	11th		Training resumed in the morning. Protection of huts in the afternoon. Still very cold.	
	12th		All ran Hamilt. inspected by Batt. fr. N.C.O. "A G" Warry inspection battn. R.E. N.C.O. B.C.D. Rout Mach.	

WAR DIARY
INTELLIGENCE SUMMARY
(Erase heading not required.)

Army Form C. 2118.

Place	Date	Hour	Summary of Events and Information	Remarks and references to Appendices
BEAUCOURT SUR JERICHO CAMP	Jan 13		Annual Church Service. Trans Commenced.	S.M.
	14th		Old Coy's detail taken to the for Church. C Coy wing & Musketry. A B D Bombing Rifle Grenade Troop Line & Physical Training.	S.M.
	15th		Major Hd M.C. having just returned from a few days leave lectured all Officers on the subject at 5 P.M. All Ranks put through the FODEN Box. D Coy using Musketry. A B C Musketry.	S.M.
	16.		Winter very bad. Heavy Rain. Bath & Batt at SUGAR Factory BEAULINCOURT. Waterproof. Flammen for demonstration at 2.30 P.M in vicinity of Camp.	S.M.
	17		Draft of 134 O.R's arrived from Depot Batt, almost entirely composed of boys of 19. L.O.C's inspection of camp at 3 P.M. Batt Concert at the Cinema Hall. SUGAR Factory at 6 P.M. Coy Training in The attack. C.O's Inspection of his Batt. Men well equipped & smart appearance. Football match against 6/I Field Ambulance. Batt lost by 3-1.	S.M.

WAR DIARY
or
INTELLIGENCE SUMMARY.
(Erase heading not required.)

Army Form C. 2118.

Place	Date	Hour	Summary of Events and Information	Remarks and references to Appendices
BEAULINCOURT R45/C'92	Jan 18th		Lt Col S.F.P. WESTON left X AMIENS on 74 ng from. Capt L.M. GLASSON DSO assumed command. Brigade 2nd in Comd was on the view. S.P. GUÉDECOURT.	
JERICHO Camp	19th		Batt was in Brigade Reserve. Batt concert in the evening from 6 P.M. & 8 P.M. Coy training and Coy amusements. All fear with rushed with great preparations to Jany into the Line.	
	20th		Batt team played Hood Brigade Football team Very easily won. Divine Sunday Services. Major HOLE MC returned from the deep leave & assumed Command. 1st Cross match Cpl H.L.I. Result drawn 1-1. Training Programme continued. All Coy Hunt Lewis Rifle Grenade & his Staff trades from 10 A.M. & 1 P.M.	
	21st		Bn of officer attended his Grace in the CINEMA HALL. 2nd Lt W.H. COTTON joined Batt & posted to 'C' Coy.	
	22nd		Capt F.S. BEAUFORD joined Batt from 1st Army School of Instruction & was posted to D Coy. Battalion marched to ROCQUIGNY Station and entrained for TRESCAULT. On detraining they marched via BEAUCAMP to relieve 'DRAKE' Battalion 63 Division, and occupied the position of Support Battalion in the left Brigade Sector (LA VACQUERIE LEFT). Relief carried out satisfactorily without casualties. Trenches very muddy. Battalion 10 pk accommodated in Inadequate TRANSPORT covered to FINS (V 6 d central)	

WAR DIARY
INTELLIGENCE SUMMARY

Army Form C. 2118.

Place	Date	Hour	Summary of Events and Information	Remarks and references to Appendices
Support Battn LAVACQUERIE LEFT Ref 57 C.20.2	Jan 23	2 AM	"A" Company occupying RHONDDA TRENCH (L.8.c.2.6) is heavily shelled. Fortunately only one casualty. Commanding Officer obtains consent to move company from this exposed position to billets + tillies in VILLERS PLOUICH. A Lewis gun is detached in this village. Two company cookers are brought up. Good water supply from well in VILLERS PLOUICH. Battalion employed by night carrying for Right Battalion Left Brigade. Movement by day restricted as enemy has good direct observation from BONNELIEU, and high ground East by CAMBRAI.	f.f.
		6 P.M	Battalion continues carrying large quantities of Bombs, S.A.A. + R.E. material for use for Battalions in Front Line Left Brigade sector. Little opposition. Apparatus for improving trenches occupied. Commanding Officers reconnoitre Right Battalion Left Brigade De Smaller Reconnaissance by O.C. companies. Battalion relieves 2nd Bttn R. Fusiliers in the night Battalion Left Brigade Sub. (LAVACQUERIE LEFT). Front line right "A" company, left "B" company. Support line right "D" coy.	f.f.
	JAN 24		Battn H.Q.rs in reserve (R.14.b.05.85). Relief carried out over the open. Front line trenches impassable. Battalion occupied carrying parties with day standings and issuing Enemy showed a distinct tendency to	f.f.
	Jan 25			

Army Form C. 2118.

WAR DIARY
or
INTELLIGENCE SUMMARY.
(Erase heading not required.)

Instructions regarding War Diaries and Intelligence Summaries are contained in F. S. Regs., Part II. and the Staff Manual respectively. Title pages will be prepared in manuscript.

Place	Date	Hour	Summary of Events and Information	Remarks and references to Appendices
Ref. LA VACQUERIE 1/10,000 Right Batt. Left Bury Sn LA VACQUERIE	Jan 25 cont'd		Every effort was made by all ranks to discourage this activity on his part with success.	f/4
	Jan 26th		Weather continued fine, intensely cold, frost carried up to front line at about 4 ft intervals throughout the night to front line. Hot food containers left in end post for consumption during daylight hours. Work concentrated on digging large dump pits in rear of front & support lines. Excellent progress made. Enemy posts located by officer patrols.	f/4
	Jan 27th		Dump pits continued. Twelve dump posts and fire steps established in front line. Heavy Regt. Support Company went forward throughout.	j/4
	Jan 28th		Battalion is relieved by 13th Essex Regt. 80 cms of trench feet during this very period in front line trenches. Battalion moved to billets in METZ via horse show country. Harassing reconnoitred by officer, recorded shelled area. Relief carried out successfully without casualties various teams 11.45 pm.	j/4
METZ	Jan 29th		Cleaning up. Inspection of clothes, equipment etc trench stores.	3/4
	Jan 30th		Port Battalion tattler at METZ. Working parties found for work on S.A.A. dump at (Q.20.b.3.7) and under party by R.E., and in building passen huts for outrchers.	3/4

A 7092 W.W.725 9/M 2597. 960,000. 1917. D.D.&L., Ltd. Forms/C.2118/14.

Army Form C. 2118.

WAR DIARY
or
INTELLIGENCE SUMMARY.
(Erase heading not required.)

Instructions regarding War Diaries and Intelligence Summaries are contained in F. S. Regs., Part II. and the Staff Manual respectively. Title pages will be prepared in manuscript.

Place	Date	Hour	Summary of Events and Information	Remarks and references to Appendices
Avesnes Rouen METZ	Jan 30th 1919		Thorupont, still lying at METZ is heavily tented. Many casualties in neighbouring units. One horse disposed on away from here, 20 casualties.	A.1.
	Jan 31st		Whilst battalion engaged in work on the METZ DEFENCES. During lunches and evenings. In the afternoon the Rgtl football XI played the 52nd Lyt INFANTRY and a hardly contested matches resulted in a win for the 52nd by 2 goals to 1. RATION STRENGTH 22 Officers and 562 Other Ranks Killed Officers nil. O.R. one Wounded Officers nil. O.R. nil	A.1.

J. H. C. Major
Cmdg. 17 th Royal Fusiliers

www.ingramcontent.com/pod-product-compliance
Lightning Source LLC
Chambersburg PA
CBHW081411160426
43193CB00013B/2151